From the Beginning: God's Salvation Plan

Joel C. Seifert

John C. Seifert

Michael J. Seifert

NORTHWESTERN PUBLISHING HOUSE
Milwaukee, Wisconsin

Northwestern Publishing House
N16W23379 Stone Ridge Dr., Waukesha, WI 53188
www.nph.net

Published 2025
Printed in the United States of America
ISBN 978-0-8100-3231-6
ISBN 978-0-8100-3232-3 (e-book)

25 26 27 28 29 30 31 32 33 34 10 9 8 7 6 5 4 3 2 1

Contents

Introduction

The People's Bible Devotions series encompasses all the books of the Bible, taking readers into devotional thoughts from Genesis through Revelation. The authors did not write a meditation on every chapter and verse in the Bible, and yet as you read through the series, you will be walking devotionally through the major sections and themes of every book in God's Holy Library.

The book you are holding presents the powerful words of God for your spiritual reflection and growth. Have a Bible or Bible app handy, because each devotion will provide a suggested reading from the Bible as context and then focus your meditation on a specific thought from our Lord in that reading. Where you notice verses and chapters not included in these devotions, accept this encouragement to read these sections of Scripture on your own, since they were inspired by the Holy Spirit and are desirable for growth, guidance, and strength.

Except for one volume, each book of this series is written by a team of authors connected to each other in some way, often as family members. Every author comes to the task with deep training in the Scriptures and rich experience in the public ministry.

This volume is based on the Pentateuch, or the first five books of the Bible. In Hebrew it is called the Torah, a word meaning "law" or "instruction." While these first five books may give a lot of attention to the laws that God gave the people of Israel in the Old Testament, the gospel is also reflected in the sacrifices and worship that God commanded. Even more important, these books trace the promise of a Savior through the lives of God's people, from the beginning in Eden to the time that God led his people into the Promised Land. The authors of these devotions will help you find the gospel revealed in the Pentateuch.

Treasure the Bible-based, Christ-centered messages you find here, inspirational for you and countless more in any place or time.

Editor

The authors of this book are John, Michael, and Joel Seifert. John is the father, and Michael and Joel are his sons. John served Good Shepherd Lutheran Church in Midland, Michigan. For over half of his ministry there, he also served as president of the Michigan District of the Wisconsin Synod (WELS). He retired in 2018. Michael served at Luther Preparatory School in Watertown, Wisconsin, and then at Living Hope Lutheran Church in Midlothian, Virginia. He is currently president of the WELS North Atlantic District. Joel served at Arizona Lutheran Academy in Phoenix; Calvary Lutheran Church in Thiensville, Wisconsin; Shining Mountains Lutheran Church in Bozeman, Montana; and is currently at Beautiful Savior Lutheran Church in Marietta, Georgia.

A Good Beginning

Bible Reading: Genesis 1:1-13

In the beginning God created the heavens and the earth. (Genesis 1:1)

It's a good sentence—a good beginning.

Here there's nothing of the "creation myths" of the ancient Near East, where gods fight and die and a new world is made out of their corpses. It's so different from the indigenous tale of a divine spider woman helping the first humans crawl out of an underground world into a place of mud and light. It has nothing in common with the stories of scientism that imagine an uncaused and unguided explosion of chaos somehow creating a beautiful and orderly cosmos.

Instead, there's just God, alone in his holiness. But he doesn't remain alone. He speaks a world into existence. We use words to describe things—to define reality as best as we can. But when God speaks, his words don't define or describe. God's words create. Things are so because he says they're so.

And they're good. When God tells us how he created the world, he isn't telling us just what the beginning was like or what the world is like. He's telling us what he's like. He's eternal—uncaused and existing before anything else. He's powerful—so powerful he can speak everything into being. And he's loving. The world that he creates isn't a place of earthquakes and hurricanes, cancers or viruses. It's a place of startling beauty and happy coexistence: humans living in blessed harmony with creation and God living in blessed peace with humans.

It's a good beginning that speaks of a good God. Throughout the pages of Scripture, we find so much pain and loss, sin and death. We find the same things in our own lives and in the world as it is now. So let this glimpse of the beginning remind us of what God is like: He wants only good for us. When we see that, it helps us understand and believe the promise he makes. Though the world has fallen in humankind's sin and so much is bad, the story of God's world will end well. The God who made this world will keep his promise to redeem and renew it through Christ Jesus.

What's waiting ahead is good. Of course it is. Because that's what God is like. He's good. You can see it even from the very beginning.

Prayer: Loving Father, through your word you created all things. By your word, create and strengthen faith in my heart so that I may always know you as my good and loving Maker. Amen.

J.C.S.

For further reading, see The People's Bible commentary on Genesis, pages 9-19.

The Image of God

Bible Reading: Genesis 1:14-31

Then God said, "Let us make mankind in our image, in our likeness, so that they may rule over the fish in the sea and the birds in the sky, over the livestock and all the wild animals, and over all the creatures that move along the ground."

27 So God created mankind in his own image, in the image of God he created them; male and female he created them. (Genesis 1:26-27)

A man finds the perfect spot. He marks boundaries and lays a floor. He builds walls and adds a roof to protect his structure from the elements. He's built a temple. In the center of it, he sets up a statue, an idol. The idol stands there deaf and mute—unable to see, hear, answer, or help. It may be fashioned in the form of a fish or eagle or monkey, but most often man makes the idol look like himself. Man seeks to make a god in his own image. But the result is weak and helpless.

Now watch God at work. He creates a beautiful world out of nothing. He sets boundaries for the sea and fills the land with goodness. He spreads the heavens above and dots the evening sky with starry light. And as his work of creation draws to a close, he too sets an image in the center of it. Not weak or sad, deaf or mute, but a living, breathing image of God, created to bless and care for God's creation. God makes humans in his image so we can be like him, blessing his world.

Remembering what we were meant to be condemns us. It highlights how selfish and self-centered we are, how intent we can be on simply serving ourselves. We may not be deaf or mute, but we're no longer the blessing our Creator intended.

But this isn't just a reminder of who we were. St. Paul reminds us that in Christ Jesus we are daily being "renewed in knowledge in the image of [our] Creator" (Colossians 3:10). This is who we, in Christ Jesus, are and will be.

Prayer: Heavenly Father, you created us to bear your image in this world. Fallen and sinful as we are, grant us forgiveness and renewal in Christ. And in his newness, use us to bless your world still. Amen.

J.C.S.

For further reading, see The People's Bible commentary on Genesis, pages 19-28.

Improving Perfection

Bible Reading: Genesis 2:1-25

The Lord God said, "It is not good for the man to be alone. I will make a helper suitable for him." (Genesis 2:18)

"God saw that it was good" (Genesis 1:10). Day by day, that refrain is repeated in the creation account. The Lord looks at what he has made and sees that it is good—good light, good land, and good seas; good animals walk through good forests while good birds fly through good skies. And when God calls these things good, he isn't just saying "good enough." His creation is perfect.

Then the Lord steps into his perfect creation. He kneels in the good dirt of Eden and makes a man in his own image. A perfect man in a perfect world. But then the Lord says, "It is not good."

"It is not good for the man to be alone." Adam is perfect, to be sure. Perfect, but not complete. From the beginning the Lord created us to show love for others. He didn't design us to be independent. Even in our perfection, we were designed to need others. And so he creates woman as a "helper suitable" for Adam—not a servant for him to command but a partner who makes him complete.

That's worth thinking about. From the very beginning, God intended marriage to make a perfect world even better. What a far cry from what we so often see today! We don't live in Eden. We live as fallen people in a fallen world, and we bring our fallenness to marriage too. We view it as a means to make ourselves happy rather than as a means to find meaning and joy in loving another. It's common and easy to assume that the problem is with marriage itself, as opposed to a problem with our sinfulness. But that's not true.

When God brings Eve to Adam, the man bursts into a song of praise. That sets a good example for us. Marriage in a fallen world is touched by pain and marked by sinfulness. But remember God's plan. We're made to need one another, designed to give and receive love. That's not weakness; that's completeness. View marriage as a chance to show love and care for your spouse. If marriage was designed to improve perfection, God can still use it to bring blessings and joy to you.

Prayer: Thank you, Lord, for our incompleteness. Thank you for our need to be loved and our need to love. Grant your blessing on all marriages. Guide and guard husband and wife, and use the marriage relationship to bring your gifts to a fallen world. Amen.

J.C.S.

For further reading, see The People's Bible commentary on Genesis, pages 28-43.

It's All Your Fault

Bible Reading: Genesis 3:1-13

The man said, "The woman you put here with me—she gave me some fruit from the tree, and I ate it."
13 Then the LORD God said to the woman, "What is this you have done?"
The woman said, "The serpent deceived me, and I ate." (Genesis 3:12-13)

"Eve was framed." Maybe you've seen that slogan. But Scripture doesn't let us get away with games like that.

God makes it clear. When the Lord God goes walking in the garden in the cool of the day, he talks to Adam and asks Adam a question: "Have you eaten from the tree that I commanded you not to eat from?" (3:11). The "you" is singular. God emphasizes that Adam was the one entrusted with God's command. And he also makes it clear that when Eve listened to the serpent and ate, Adam "was with her" (3:6). God had commanded Adam. He didn't obey. Satan had tempted Eve. She listened.

So whose fault was it? Adam's or Eve's? That's the game they played. The husband looked at the wife he was to love and care for and instead saw a tool to help him get out of trouble: "It's all her fault!" Eve pointed to the one who tempted her as though she had no ability to do what was right: "It's all his fault!"

Whose fault was it? Everyone was right. Read the pages of the New Testament and you'll read that sin entered the world through Adam (Romans 5:12) and that Eve was the one who was deceived (1 Timothy 2:14). The fall into sin is attributed to both of them. It's like most marriages and most problems today: There's plenty of blame to go around.

Whose fault is it? That question doesn't divide just husbands and wives, lifelong friends, or members of a church. It also distracts us from what's taking place whenever there's a call to repentance. Why was God walking in the garden in the cool of the day, calling to them? He wasn't calling them to punish them; he was calling them to repentance so he could forgive them.

Adam and Eve missed this call. Let's be sure we don't. When problems arise and blame seeks to divide us, don't get distracted. Be quick to own your part in every problem, confess your sins, and rejoice in God's forgiveness.

Prayer: Lord Jesus, you bore my guilt on the tree. Instead of hiding from my sin, help me freely confess it and, as a forgiven sinner, share your forgiveness with those who hurt me too. Amen.

J.C.S.

For further reading, see The People's Bible commentary on Genesis, pages 43-51.

Not Good, but Never Abandoned

Bible Reading: Genesis 3:14-24

"I will put enmity
between you and the woman,
and between your offspring and hers;
he will crush your head,
and you will strike his heel." (Genesis 3:15)

The first promise of the coming Savior was spoken to the serpent. God's promise of deliverance and blessing for his fallen people was spoken as a curse against the devil. The promise wasn't filled with the refrain of "good . . . good . . . good" that echoed through God's creation of the world. It couldn't have been. The world was no longer the good place God had created it to be. Instead, the promise was filled with enmity and violence as a champion from God would come to do war. But even in that, the promise would be filled with Christ. Have you considered how much of Jesus is in these words?

God didn't give Adam and Eve a plan for how they might restore their relationship with him. In fact, he didn't tell them to do anything. He was going to be the one providing a champion.

This champion, sent from God, would be born of a woman—sent by and from God, yet at the same time human. And the promise added a strange-sounding detail: English translations generally talk about Eve's "offspring," but the original Hebrew talks of Eve's "seed." How bizarre! Hebrew doesn't usually speak of the "seed" of a woman; "seed" is associated with the father. It doesn't make much sense—unless this coming seed would have no earthly father, but only a mother.

And this champion would do battle, destroying the work of the serpent in our place—crushing his head! But even though victorious, the champion would still suffer, being struck in return.

In so many ways, it was a brutal promise. It spoke of hatred and war, ongoing generations of violence and struggle and death. No wonder there was no "it was good." Things weren't good, not yet. But in the words of the promise, God pointed to the day he would send his heavenly champion, born of a woman, with no human father, who would suffer for us as he destroyed the devil. In God's promise, you aren't abandoned. Things aren't good, but you're not alone. Things aren't perfect, but they will be again one day.

Prayer: Lord, from the very first day of the fall into sin, you pointed sinners to Christ. As we see your promise of love in the beginning, help us remember that you'll love us to the end. Amen.

J.C.S.

For further reading, see The People's Bible commentary on Genesis, pages 51-58.

The First Broken Family

Bible Reading: Genesis chapter 4

Adam made love to his wife Eve, and she became pregnant and gave birth to Cain. She said, "With the help of the Lord I have brought forth a man." [2] Later she gave birth to his brother Abel.

Now Abel kept flocks, and Cain worked the soil. (Genesis 4:1-2)

Cain made love to his wife, and she became pregnant and gave birth to Enoch. Cain was then building a city, and he named it after his son Enoch. (Genesis 4:17)

Seth also had a son, and he named him Enosh.

At that time people began to call on the name of the Lord. (Genesis 4:26)

God had made a promise. Surely when Eve gave birth to her first son, this crossed her mind: "With painful labor you will give birth to children" (Genesis 3:16). But still, what a gift. Her cries of pain gave way to tears of joy. In a world marked by death, new life still emerged. She really was the mother of all the living.

And there had been another promise. Her offspring, the Lord God had said, would crush the serpent's head. As she held baby Cain tightly against her chest, she wondered if he might be the one. Not just her son—her Savior.

But when he grew up, it was not the serpent's head he crushed. It was his brother's. Oh, to be the mother! A horror she could not have imagined fulfilled another word of God: "You will surely die." Abel's blood, spilled by Cain's hand, cried out from the ground. Part of Eve died with Abel, but she had to go on living. Jealousy, hatred, violence, murder, and brokenness in families are nothing new. Everything goes back to the very first family. Sin has taken hold of the human heart down through the generations.

Sin's grip on Cain was strong. Instead of repenting of it, he groused about the consequences. God sentenced him to restless wandering, but Cain doubled down on his defiance and built a city. God had warned him, "Sin is crouching at your door" (4:7), and Cain invited the sin inside. It made a home in his heart. It ruled over him. Eve lost two sons.

But God would keep his promise. Eve's offspring would crush the devil's head. Even as Abel's blood cried out from the ground, even as Cain shrugged off his restless wandering and anchored himself in place on the foundations of his city, the Lord still provided. Again, Eve's painful labor gave way to joy. Seth wasn't the Savior either, but follow his offspring down the line and you'll come to a manger in Bethlehem. Follow his offspring down the line and you'll also see God at work preserving a remnant of believers with his name on their lips: "At that time people began to call on the name of the LORD" (4:26).

Eve's family was broken. But God can make something whole even from broken families. Through her broken family, God would bring healing for all the broken. He had made a promise, and that promise would never be broken.

Prayer: Lord God, you instituted family to be a source of so much blessing. But our sin has also caused it to be the source of so much pain. I pray that you bring healing to broken families through your Son's forgiveness. Let his love shine brightly in our homes. Amen.

M.J.S.

For further reading, see The People's Bible commentary on Genesis, pages 58-67.

And Then He Died

Bible Reading: Genesis chapter 5

When Adam had lived 130 years, he had a son in his own likeness, in his own image; and he named
him Seth. 4After Seth was born, Adam lived 800
years and had other sons and daughters. 5Altogether,
Adam lived a total of 930 years, and then he died.
(Genesis 5:3-5)

Methuselah holds the record—969 years. That's what readers tend to take away from Genesis chapter 5. How could the people live so long? Some have wondered if the physical environment before the flood was friendlier to human life. It's plausible. After that worldwide catastrophe, lifespans were decidedly shorter (see Genesis 11:10-26).

Whatever physical or environmental factors were at play, we know that God was the ultimate cause of their sky-high ages. But *why* did they live so long? While the Bible doesn't provide a definitive answer to that question, we can identify at least two blessings he provided through their longevity.

The first blessing was that the earth could be quickly filled, just as God blessed and commanded Adam and Eve to do when he created them. People weren't just living for a long time. Each generation was having children for a long time. Lamech was 182 when he had Noah. After that, he lived another 595 years and had other sons and daughters. We don't know the world's population at the time of the flood, but there was enough childbearing capacity for it to have easily rivaled today's.

The second blessing was that the promise could be passed on. For 930 years, Adam was around to tell more than 20 generations of his descendants what God had promised when he and Eve turned their backs on him: "He will crush your head, and you will strike his heel" (Genesis 3:15). For almost a thousand years, there was an eyewitness to the gospel. And after Adam died, there were so many eyewitnesses of the eyewitness. It's possible that Adam was still alive when Methuselah was born. It's possible that Methuselah was still alive when God sent the flood. The people's longevity gave the gospel time to get a foothold.

But if their longevity is our only takeaway here, we're missing something big. Almost every paragraph of chapter 5 ends with the same four words: "and then he died." Living 969 years is unfathomable. But it's infinitely shorter than the lifespan God had intended for humankind at the beginning when he made them in the likeness of God. This genealogy from Adam to Noah reads like a funeral toll. Every ring of the bell is a jolting reminder of God's promise to Adam and to all who are born in *his* likeness, *his* image: "Dust you are and to dust you will return" (Genesis 3:19).

But until the bell tolled for each generation, God was providing the people time to pass on the promise through which he overcomes death. Eve's offspring was on his way: "The wages of sin is death, but the gift of God is eternal life in Christ Jesus our Lord" (Romans 6:23).

Prayer: Father in heaven, make me aware of my own mortality and its cause. Send your Spirit to teach me to hold on to Jesus for real life that never ends. For as many days as you give me on this earth, use me as your Spirit's instrument to pass on his promise of life to others. Amen.

M.J.S.

For further reading, see The People's Bible commentary on Genesis, pages 68-73.

The Lord's Love Never Sits Still

Bible Reading: Genesis 6:1-8

The LORD saw how great the wickedness of the human race had become on the earth, and that every inclination of the thoughts of the human heart was only evil all the time. 6 The LORD regretted that he had made human beings on the earth, and his heart was deeply troubled. (Genesis 6:5-6)

"For God so loved the world . . . " (John 3:16). Those words are more precious than rubies. When God looks down on a world turned away from him and turned against itself, his reaction is love! And his love springs into action: " . . . that he gave his one and only Son." God's love is for all, and his love never sits still.

But sin never sits still either. Like cancer, its nature is to grow and destroy. Left untreated, that's what it always does.

Adam thought, "What's a bite of fruit going to hurt?" Cain let his anger rule over him. Even as the gospel promise was passed down through the generations, many shrugged it off. God's people traded in love for lust. Where God saw wickedness, they saw beauty. Faith wasn't a factor in their marriages. And so in the days before the flood, faith in the serpent-crusher was being bred out of existence. Their sins may have seemed small to them, but they weren't seeing clearly. Sin was putting its foot in the door of their hearts. Left untreated, it moved in and reigned supreme.

"The Lord saw" not only how widespread sin and unbelief were across humanity. He saw how intense these things were in the individual human heart. Every inclination was only evil all the time. You cannot squeeze a single drop of goodness out of a sin-filled heart.

"The Lord saw" and "the Lord regretted." That doesn't sound right. God doesn't make mistakes. True, God hadn't done anything wrong. There were no flaws baked into his creation, which makes it even more of a tragedy. The crown of God's creation turned away from him and against itself. To express God's reaction in terms of a human emotion, it broke his heart. To express it in terms of God's love that never sits still, he was about to spring into action.

He would wipe the human race from the face of the earth. Anyone who thinks that's too harsh isn't seeing clearly. The cancer had to be cut out. No doubt about it, there's judgment here. Just remember: God's judgment serves his love.

God remembered his promise. That's why he sent the flood. He would preserve a remnant of humanity to bring the Savior. He would preserve a remnant of believers to pass on the promise of the Savior. But his love would not allow sin to go untreated.

Prayer: Create in me a pure heart, O God. You alone can do it. Do not take your Holy Spirit from me. Let him dwell in me with power so that I trust in your forgiveness, wage war against temptation, and shine as a beacon of your love in this dark world. Amen.

M.J.S.

For further reading, see The People's Bible commentary on Genesis, pages 73-76.

God Destroys the World to Save It

Bible Reading: Genesis 6:9–8:14

"I will establish my covenant with you, and you will enter the ark—you and your sons and your wife and your sons' wives with you." (Genesis 6:18)

Every living thing on the face of the earth was wiped out; people and animals and the creatures that move along the ground and the birds were wiped from the earth. Only Noah was left, and those with him in the ark. (Genesis 7:23)

God's description of the flood is mostly matter of fact—things like durations and depths and the inhabitants of the ark. There's no mention of the masses clamoring toward high ground, pushing and screaming and dragging each other under, or the sudden silence when the last set of lungs filled with water. It's just matter of fact: "Every living thing on the face of the earth was wiped out" (7:23). There were no search parties holding out hope. Everything that lived on land was dead. Gory details aren't required for this to strike the fear of God into our hearts. Matter of fact is awful enough.

It brings to mind a line from an old hymn: "If you think of sin but lightly nor suppose the evil great" (CW 430:3). In the flood we witness the gravity of the sins that don't even make us blush anymore. This is what happens when God's patience runs out. He cuts out the cancer. It's exactly what he said he'd do.

But look! A wooden box the size of a football field was bobbing on the surface of the same water that wiped out the earth. There was more to God's promise than destruction. It was inside that box. "Everything on earth will perish," God had said to Noah, "but I will establish my covenant with you" (Genesis 6:17-18). Through Noah, God would still keep his promise to send the serpent-crusher.

We might tend to think of the flood as judgment. It was judgment: God's patience had come to an end, and he unleashed his wrath against the wicked. But there's another side to that coin: a big wooden box bobbing along the waves with eight people to whom God had made a promise. He would preserve their faith in that promise even though it required covering the earth with miles of water.

The centerpiece of this passage isn't God's righteous wrath against the wicked—even though that's here. It's not the faith of Noah within an unbelieving generation—even though that's also here. The centerpiece is God's promise: "I will establish my covenant with you." God had a Savior to send, and nothing was going to stop him from doing it—not even all the evil in the world.

Prayer: Savior Jesus, enlighten my heart to know the true nature of my sin. May it always make me blush with shame so I may stand in awe of your boundless and determined love—love that called my sin your own and that suffered and died so I might live and delight in you. Amen.

M.J.S.

For further reading, see The People's Bible commentary on Genesis, pages 77-89.

A Flood Can't Take Away the Sin of the World

Bible Reading: Genesis 8:15–9:17

"Never again will I curse the ground because of humans, even though every inclination of the human heart is evil from childhood." (Genesis 8:21)

14 "Whenever I bring clouds over the earth and the rainbow appears in the clouds, 15 I will remember my covenant between me and you and all living creatures of every kind. Never again will the waters become a flood to destroy all life." (Genesis 9:14-15)

After a year on the water, Noah and his family finally felt firm ground under their feet again. The animals scurried out, back into their God-intended habitats. Shoots of green were everywhere. It smelled like spring. Life had returned to the earth—a fresh start.

Would the second time around go better than the first? God resolved to never again send a worldwide flood—but not because the water washed the world clean of sin. He sent the flood because he saw "that every inclination of the thoughts of the human heart was only evil all the time" (Genesis 6:5). But he knew that the same evil still dwelled in the hearts of Noah and his family. Now—for the same reason he sent the flood—he determined *not* to send another flood, because "every inclination of the human heart is evil from childhood" (8:21).

It's not that the flood had failed to accomplish its purpose. It's that its purpose wasn't to take away the sin of the world. It was a stop-gap measure. God was judging the impenitent and sending a warning to all others who would follow the same path. He was preserving faith on the earth—faith in the offspring of Eve—before it went extinct. Only he could crush the serpent's head. Only he, the Lamb of God, could take away the sin of the world.

After a storm, the sun breaks through clouds. Mist in the air refracts the light like an atmospheric prism. We know the physical properties that make a rainbow happen. But we also know that God is behind it. He paints the sky as a seal of his promise. It reminds us of his mercy. And God remembers his mercy too. Never again will he send a worldwide flood. Because of God's patient mercy, planting and harvests, days and seasons will continue until the Lamb of God who has taken away the sin of the world comes again. Then in judgment and mercy he will wipe away every last trace of sin forever, and every inclination of our hearts will be only righteous all the time. He will give us a real fresh start that will never perish, spoil, or fade.

Prayer: Lord God, heavenly King, impress on my heart that Jesus is the only solution to the sin of the world, including mine. Curb the violence of the earth in line with your good purposes. Send your Spirit through your Word even more so that my heart and the hearts of many more may be ready when Jesus returns to do away with sin forever. Amen.

M.J.S.

For further reading, see The People's Bible commentary on Genesis, pages 89-97.

What Parents Give Their Children

Bible Reading: Genesis 9:18–10:32

The sons of Noah who came out of the ark were Shem, Ham and Japheth. (Ham was the father of Canaan.) 19 These were the three sons of Noah, and from them came the people who were scattered over the whole earth. (Genesis 9:18-19)

Before the flood, Noah was introduced as "a righteous man, blameless among the people of his time" (Genesis 6:9). His lifestyle testified to his faith. He walked with God. He taught his sons to do the same. These are the ancestors of everyone on earth today.

Noah's lifestyle testified to his faith, but he also committed sins that testified to his need for a Savior. So did his sons. An unsavory event began like so many others: with intoxication. Noah's drunkenness led to his nakedness. In kindness to Noah, God spares us the details.

Noah dishonored himself. Ham dishonored him further. Again, God spares us the details.

Shem and Japheth shined on a dark day. They refused to add to their father's indignity.

Even godly homes have sin inside. In that respect, our homes are like our hearts. We see the harm sin inflicts on successive generations. It's one thing to know that our children inherit our sinful nature. It's another to confess that they also learn from our sinful behavior. If only we could intervene between God and our children: "Hold me responsible, not them!" But it doesn't work that way.

This is how it works. The Christian father lets his child hear him repent: "God, have mercy on me, a sinner." He lets his child see him battle against his sinful nature so that his lifestyle testifies to his faith. The Christian mother kneels with her little ones at their bedside: "Thank you, Jesus, for dying on the cross to take away our sins. Give us a good night's rest so that we can serve you tomorrow." These parents teach their children repentance and its fruit.

The Christian parent's prayer isn't "Hold me responsible, not them!" It's "Thank you, God, for sending your Son, Jesus. Thank you for holding him responsible for my sin and my children's sin. Use me, God, to teach them to trust this and to never let go." Let us ever walk with Jesus.

Prayer: Thank you, God, for sending your Son, Jesus. Thank you for holding him responsible for my sin and for the sins of all who are in my care. Use me, God, to teach my children to trust this and to never let go. Grant that all Christian parents may do that for their children, and their children for their children, down through the generations. Amen.

M.J.S.

For further reading, see The People's Bible commentary on Genesis, pages 97-107.

God Scatters So He Might Gather

Bible Reading: Genesis 11:1-26

The LORD came down to see the city and the tower the people were building. 6The LORD said, "If as one people speaking the same language they have begun to do this, then nothing they plan to do will be impossible for them. 7Come, let us go down and confuse their language so they will not understand each other." (Genesis 11:5-7)

If only people weren't divided by race and language. If only people weren't split into nations that war and rage against each other. If only people weren't divided into haves and have-nots but had shared technology and resources. If we were all one people with one language and one land, can you imagine what we could accomplish?

Welcome to Babel. It was on a beautiful plain that reached as far as the eye could see, with enough clean water and fresh food to feed an empire. God had told humankind to spread out and fill his world with life, but Babel was the kind of place where people could really put down roots and build something. So they did. God told them to spread out, but they wanted to go up. They started to work on a tower that could reach to the skies. Humankind came together and said, "Yes! We can do anything we put our minds to and reach the top!" But God said, "Oh no. They can do anything they put their minds to and put themselves above my will."

So "the LORD came down." Don't miss that detail. Moses uses the special name "LORD" that emphasizes God's faithful love. "The LORD came down," but he was more heartbroken than angry. He gave them different languages so they would stop building on their own lies. He scattered them from one another before they were lost from him forever.

Maybe it seems like God is the troublemaker here. He scattered humankind! Now we have different languages and nations and races. But God's goal wasn't to divide us. At Babel, humankind was united in sinful rebellion against God. Pay attention through the rest of the Old Testament and you'll see God's plan in action. He'll make a promise to a Chaldean named Abram. Abram, or Abraham, will found a nation called Israel. People will come from the nations to hear about Israel's gracious God. And a Savior will give his life because God so loved the world, and God will bring people from every nation and language to find true unity in Christ. God scattered humans so we wouldn't live up to our sinful potential, but he gathers us together around the forgiveness that Jesus won.

Prayer: Almighty God, I'm tempted to think that the problems in this world come from our differences. Help me today to be mindful that the real enemy lives in my heart. Thank you for the ways you frustrate and destroy that enemy's work, even when it brings me pain. And when it does, use that pain to bring me closer to you. Amen.

J.C.S.

For further reading, see The People's Bible commentary on Genesis, pages 107-113.

Faith Isn't Blind; It Listens

Bible Reading: Genesis 12:1-9

The LORD had said to Abram, "Go from your country, your people and your father's household to the land I will show you.

2 "I will make you into a great nation,
and I will bless you;
I will make your name great,
and you will be a blessing.
3 I will bless those who bless you,
and whoever curses you I will curse;
and all peoples on earth
will be blessed through you." (Genesis 12:1-3)

"So, Abram, where are you going?"

That must have been an awkward question for Abram to answer. He had prepared his wife and servants for the journey; they had rounded up the livestock and set aside supplies; he had said farewell to his relatives. But when people asked him where he was going, he had no answer. God didn't tell Abram where he was going. God just told him he would show him the way.

When people talk about "blind faith," they miss something. Faith *never* really sees its object. If it did, it would be sight, not faith. Instead, faith trusts the promises it's been given. Faith doesn't see; it listens. Abram didn't know where he was going, but he knew the one who was leading him.

So Abram left behind the life he knew, even though he hadn't seen the land he was going to. He trusted that the Lord would make him a blessing to others, even though he saw no proof. He found comfort that God would defend him against his enemies, even though they surrounded him. He believed that all peoples on earth would be blessed through him, even though he was a childless old man. He didn't see these things; he listened to God's promises. And he followed.

And so do we. We share the gospel to bless others, even though so often we don't see results. We trust that God is using everything for our good, even though it often doesn't feel like it. And sometimes we're tempted to think we're operating on blind faith, but that's not how faith works. It is never about seeing. Faith listens, just as Abram did.

But there is one difference. As we follow God with his promises in our ears and someone asks us where we're going, we know exactly what to say: "I'm going home to heaven. God has promised."

Prayer: Dear Savior, when I don't see what you've promised me with my eyes, help me keep your promises in my ears and follow you with a listening faith. Amen.

J.C.S.

For further reading, see The People's Bible commentary on Genesis, pages 117-123.

Tents Poorly Pitched

Bible Reading: Genesis chapter 13

Abram lived in the land of Canaan, while Lot lived among the cities of the plain and pitched his tents near Sodom. [13]Now the people of Sodom were wicked and were sinning greatly against the LORD. (Genesis 13:12-13)

It was the best looking site in the whole campground. While other sites were strewn with pine cones, sticks, and rocks, this one was nothing but hard-packed earth. So I pitched my tent, looking forward to a great night's sleep.

But I didn't get that good sleep. It rained that night, and much of the water that came through the campground flowed right across the site I chose. My tent became a waterbed!

When you're making decisions that shape your life, it's easy to focus on the wrong things and miss the bigger picture. That happened to Lot. The Lord had blessed Lot and Abram so greatly that they had to split up and choose where each would live. Lot thought he had found a perfect place to call home. Moses said the plain where Lot settled was "like the garden of the LORD" (13:10)—like Eden itself! It was such a good land that Lot didn't seem troubled that he was pitching his tent next to people known for their perverse and violent sins against God. Fast-forward to Genesis chapter 19. Lot is not camped outside the city anymore. He and his family are living in a house in town. They've become warped by the sinfulness of their neighbors. When angels come to rescue them before God destroys the city, Lot and his family are not even sure they want to leave!

So what's the lesson for you and me? Stay away from sinners? Such a thing isn't possible this side of heaven. History is full of attempts by Christians to separate themselves from a sinful world. They've lived as hermits in the desert, formed monastic communities, set up governmental laws to enforce Christian behavior, and fled the "sinful cities" for "safe" country life. And whenever they have, they've realized that sin is still with them. After all, it lives in us!

What does it mean to pitch your tent well? It doesn't mean fleeing a sinful world. We follow a Savior who calls us to live in this world as salt and light, serving as witnesses of his truth, his holiness, and his love. It means we need to remember that we really are "camping." This place isn't our home. So live in the world, but don't become part of it. No matter what sin you see around you, live for God's promises. And no matter where you pitch your tent, the Lord will be with you.

Prayer: Lord of life, as I serve you today, help me consider what it means that you call me to live in the world but not to be of the world. Let my greatest joy be in your Word. Amen.

J.C.S.

For further reading, see The People's Bible commentary on Genesis, pages 126-131.

A Priestly King of Righteousness and Peace

Bible Reading: Genesis chapter 14

Then Melchizedek king of Salem brought out bread and wine. He was priest of God Most High,
19 and he blessed Abram, saying,
"Blessed be Abram by God Most High,
Creator of heaven and earth.
20 And praise be to God Most High,
who delivered your enemies into your hand."
Then Abram gave him a tenth of everything.
(Genesis 14:18-20)

Shadows are mysterious things.

If you see a shadow approaching, you can learn a few things about what's coming your way. Is it a person, a car, or an animal? Is it large or small? Moving quickly or slowly? You can learn a few things but not enough to get a full picture. Shadows give you the rough shape of things. They give you outlines.

So it is with Melchizedek. We meet Melchizedek here in Genesis chapter 14. In many ways, he's a shadow of Christ. All shadows have some mystery to them; Melchizedek has more than most. We meet him for just three verses. After a great victory in battle, he blesses Abram and receives a tenth of the plunder from him. His name means king of righteousness. He is the king of the city that will one day become Jerusalem. The book of Hebrews reminds us that "king of Salem" also means "king of peace." (Hebrews chapter 7 gives a helpful commentary on Melchizedek.) We know nothing of his ancestry; it's almost as if he has no beginning and no end. And somehow this king, not of Abram's family, was a priest of God Most High.

Do you see the image of Christ beginning to take shape? Melchizedek is a priest, yet a king. He is without beginning or end. He comes in righteousness and in peace as he serves God Most High. He comes to bless his people, and his people rejoice to give their gifts to him. He's a mysterious figure, without a doubt, but he gives us an idea of the one who was coming. In fact, in Psalm 110:4 God tells us that Jesus would be "in the order of Melchizedek." Melchizedek gives an outline.

We've seen the fullness of Christ revealed in the Scriptures; we don't need shadows or outlines anymore. So what can we learn from Melchizedek? When life seems out of control, when you don't see God's plan in any of it, remember that God's loving plan to send a Savior and deliver you has been in the works since the very beginning. God's plan has always included you. Sometimes we don't see his plan. It's mysterious; it's fuzzy; we just see outlines and shadows. So look to Jesus, and God will bring his love for you into focus.

Prayer: As I go about my day today, Lord, give me the peace of knowing that even if I don't understand your plans for me, you bring your love and will for me into focus when I think of Jesus, my righteous King of peace. Amen.

J.C.S.

For further reading, see The People's Bible commentary on Genesis, pages 131-137.

A Solid Promise for a Wavering Faith

Bible Reading: Genesis chapter 15

Abram believed the Lord, and he credited it to him as righteousness. (Genesis 15:6)

Someone once warned, "Never meet your heroes. They'll always disappoint you." That's the thing about heroes: Their stories tell of their victories and accomplishments. They don't tend to tell you about their flaws and failures.

But God tells us everything. Meet Abram. We often call him a "hero of faith." It's not hard to see why. He left his family and his country behind when God called him, even though he didn't know where he was going. He believed God's promise that the Lord would give him a new land and make him into a great nation. He trusted God in long travels and in battles against impossible odds. He had incredible faith!

And incredible flaws and incredible failures. In Genesis, we see a few of them. He lied about his wife and put her in danger to protect himself. Twice. He doubted God would keep his promise to give him a son through his wife, so he took the matter into his own hands and another woman into his own bed. In

Abram, we meet someone who one minute does amazing things and shows heroic faith, only the next minute to act in fear and doubt, weakness and sin. We meet someone who's much like me. Much like you.

If God judged Abram by his actions, he would have called him as sinful as any one of us. But here's a miracle of God's grace: God saw Abram's faith in his promises, and God credited Abram's faith as righteousness. In Abram, we see how God deals with us. Our salvation doesn't depend on the holiness of our actions. It doesn't even depend on the strength of our faith. It depends on the mercy of a God who calls us righteous through our faith in his promises.

That's why God tells us about Abram. It's not so we get to know our heroes but so we get to know God himself.

Prayer: Dear Jesus, thank you for the gift of faith you've given me. Thank you for the times it gives me strength to trust you in the face of fear or to dare to do incredible things. And for the times I doubt or fail, thank you, Jesus, for crediting even my weak faith as your perfect righteousness. Amen.

J.C.S.

For further reading, see The People's Bible commentary on Genesis, pages 137-144.

The God Who Sees Me

Bible Reading: Genesis 16

[Hagar] gave this name to the LORD who spoke to her: "You are the God who sees me," for she said, "I have now seen the One who sees me." (Genesis 16:13)

God doesn't need our help to keep his promises.

It had been more than ten years since the Lord told Abram that all the nations of the earth would be blessed through him. More than ten years of watching his old body get older. More than ten years of his wife Sarai watching each month come and go with no signs of pregnancy—or even that pregnancy was somehow possible. Ten years in and nobody was getting any younger. Abram and Sarai believed that God would keep his promise. They just thought he must need some help.

So Sarai realized something: God had said that all the nations of the earth would be blessed through Abram, but did that promise include her? Luckily, there was another option at hand. She told her husband to sleep with her slave woman and have a child with her. Just violate some of God's clearest commandments, and we can help him keep his promises!

It's sad to see how it all turned out. Sad, but not surprising. Abram committed adultery with Sarai's slave Hagar. A child was conceived. Hagar was a victim, but she wasn't innocent. She saw this growing child not just as a possible child of the promise but as a promising way to gain power over her mistress. Hagar despised Sarai; Sarai complained to Abram; Abram washed his hands of the whole thing. Sarai abused her slave, and pregnant Hagar fled into the desert.

God doesn't need our help to keep his promises. We don't need to violate his will to accomplish his plans. Yet so often we think we'll find the happiness and blessings God wants us to have by running away from the God who promises to give them.

And God sees it all. The Lord found Hagar out in the desert. He sent her back home. Life would have its hardships there. It wouldn't be perfect, but she wouldn't be alone. The Lord would be with her—and with Sarai and Abram. Hagar's son wouldn't be the child of the promise, but God would keep his promise to send a Savior for her, for them, and for the world, all by himself. He doesn't need our help. He simply calls for our faith.

Prayer: Thank you, Lord, for keeping your promises in spite of me. Help me, Lord, to trust in you. Amen.

J.C.S.

For further reading, see The People's Bible commentary on Genesis, pages 144-149.

A Sign in the Flesh to Encourage Faith in the Heart

Bible Reading: Genesis 17

Then God said to Abraham, "As for you, you must keep my covenant, you and your descendants after you for the generations to come. [10]This is my covenant with you and your descendants after you, the covenant you are to keep: Every male among you shall be circumcised. [11]You are to undergo circumcision, and it will be the sign of the covenant between me and you." (Genesis 17:9-11)

God made a covenant with Abraham. A covenant is a contract, a promise. The Lord promised Abraham that he would make him into a great nation, living in a rich land. When God promised to bless the world through Abraham, he was promising to send a Savior through Abraham's family. But you know what can happen when people make us promises. We can begin to doubt them. We can forget what others have promised us or wonder if the promises will really come true.

So God gave Abraham a "sign" of the covenant: circumcision. God commanded that Abraham and all the males in his household after him be circumcised. But the act of circumcision didn't earn Abraham a right relationship with God. In the book of Romans, the apostle Paul points out that God had already credited Abraham as righteous through faith long before he was circumcised (Romans 4:9-11). Circumcision was to be a daily, visible reminder in Abraham's flesh of the promise God had made to him. And God wanted that sign given to each generation because he wanted the promise of a Savior passed on from generation to generation.

God tells us that circumcision isn't necessary for believers anymore, but there are important lessons for us to consider here. At times—even in the New Testament church—people have thought that the outward act of circumcision was what gave them a right relationship with God. So both in the Old Testament and New Testament, God tells us that he wants us to "circumcise" our hearts—that is, to look to God in true repentance and faith (Deuteronomy 10:16; Romans 2:29). Circumcision itself isn't what matters; true faith expressing itself through love matters (Galatians 5:6).

Outward signs can be a blessing. Maybe you treasure a cross necklace that you wear or a certificate on your wall from the day you were baptized. Such things can give us daily reminders of God's grace to us. And we need to let them be just that: not something outward that we put our confidence in but reminders of God's promises about our Savior.

Prayer: Lord Jesus, thank you for your precious promises and for the things in my life that daily remind me of your grace. Amen.

J.C.S.

For further reading, see The People's Bible commentary on Genesis, pages 149-157.

When There Aren't Even Ten

Bible Reading: Genesis 18:16-33

Then [Abraham] said, "May the Lord not be angry, but let me speak just once more. What if only ten can be found there?"

He answered, "For the sake of ten, I will not destroy it." (Genesis 18:32)

Abraham is often used as an example of how to pray. When the Lord tells Abraham that he's about to destroy the city where Abraham's nephew lives, Abraham begins his prayer. He asks the Lord to spare the city if 50 righteous people can be found there. The Lord agrees. But Abraham doesn't stop there. Five times he goes back to God with his request, each time asking for a little more grace until the Lord agrees to spare the cities of Sodom and Gomorrah if only ten righteous people are found there.

We can learn a lot about prayer from this account. Abraham is bold; he's not afraid to bring big requests to God that would change the Lord's plans. Abraham appeals to God's character; he prays with trust in God's righteousness and mercy. Abraham is humble; he recognizes that he's a mere mortal bringing requests to an almighty God. And Abraham's prayer is answered; God agrees to spare the cities if only ten righteous people are found.

But the cities are still destroyed. The next chapter makes it clear that even ten righteous people couldn't be found in the cities, and destruction rains down from heaven.

Even in that there is something important to learn about prayer. We can pray with all trust in God's mercy and in all humility. We can ask him for good and gracious blessings. And even when his answer is yes, it won't always look the way we hope. Sometimes the sin is so deep or the evil is so complete that the most loving thing God can do is send punishment. Sometimes the world is so broken that the greatest deliverance he can give is to bring us out of this life. Maybe the marriage ends, the loved one is swallowed by their sin, or the cancer spreads.

But that doesn't mean God isn't listening or that his answer isn't loving. It may be just a reflection of how sinful and broken the world is. So learn a lesson from Abraham. Pray boldly, pray with confidence and humility, and know that God is answering you, even when it doesn't feel like it.

Prayer: In a broken world, your love, O Lord, is unfailing. Help me trust in your righteousness and grace. Help me to be faithful in prayer, knowing that you are always faithful in your answers. Amen.

J.C.S.

For further reading, see The People's Bible commentary on Genesis, pages 161-165.

Convicted by the Guilty

Bible Reading: Genesis chapter 20

Then Abimelek called Abraham in and said, "What have you done to us? How have I wronged you that you have brought such great guilt upon me and my kingdom? You have done things to me that should never be done." [10] And Abimelek asked Abraham, "What was your reason for doing this?" (Genesis 20:9-10)

God tells us that one day believers will judge the world (1 Corinthians 6:2). Yet sometimes God uses the world to judge us.

Abraham acted like a coward. While he was living in a new land, he was afraid that the people of that place would kill him so they could take his wife for themselves. So he devised a plan: He told everyone that Sarah was his sister, not his wife. The king then took her for himself. Abraham, the follower of the true God, spoke in lies. The one who trusted God's promises acted in fear. The father-to-be of God's people showed neither love nor respect for his wife. It all made sense to him: The people of that region were wicked unbelievers, so of course he needed to do this evil thing to protect himself.

Abraham was wrong, and the Lord used the pagan king Abimelek to convict him. God not only kept Abimelek from sinning with Sarah, he also acknowledged that Abimelek acted with a clean conscience. Abimelek didn't know he'd taken a married woman. The sin was Abraham's.

Believers can fall into an easy temptation: We can assume that unbelievers will always act immorally and that our actions are then justified. Abraham thought that. Do you ever think that? Are you quick to think the worst about the world around you? It's a shameful thing when believers use their own faith as a reason to look down on unbelieving friends, to slander unchristian leaders, or to refuse help for those in need because of the assumptions we might have about them.

Abraham's cowardly and sinful actions came from his self-righteous assumptions about others. He was blind to his own sin, so the Lord used a pagan king to convict him. Take that lesson to heart. Don't use assumptions about unbelievers to justify your own immoral actions. And if the Lord should use the unbelieving world to point out your own sinfulness, let the people around you see how a child of God acts: Repent, receive the Lord's forgiveness with trust and thanksgiving, and seek to repair the damage you've done.

Prayer: Dear Savior, you call us to live as your righteous people in a fallen world. When I exchange your righteousness for my own self-righteousness, lovingly correct and restore me so that I may show your grace to others. Amen.

J.C.S.

For further reading, see The People's Bible commentary on Genesis, pages 172-176.

God Doesn't Hide From the Hurt

Bible Reading: Genesis 21:1–22:3

Then God said, "Take your son, your only son, whom you love—Isaac—and go to the region of Moriah. Sacrifice him there as a burnt offering on a mountain I will show you." (Genesis 22:2)

When God calls us to a life of faith, he asks for more than we can imagine. And he knows how much it can hurt us.

Believers struggle with the account of God calling Abraham to sacrifice Isaac. Abraham had sacrificed before. He knew what God was telling him to do. God told Abraham to tie up his son, slaughter him like an animal, and burn his body until it was nothing but ash. How could God tell him to do such a thing? Didn't God know how hard this must have been for Abraham?

God knew. He didn't hide from how much he was asking Abraham to sacrifice: "Take your son, your only son, whom you love—Isaac."

We know that the Bible is the message of God's love for the world, so maybe this detail surprises us: The first time the Bible uses the Hebrew word for love isn't when God created the world. It isn't when he united Adam and Eve in the first marriage. It isn't even the first time that he promised to send a Savior into the world. It's here, as God describes the emotion that Abraham has for his only son—right as God tells Abraham to kill Isaac. *Your only son, whom you love.*

When God tests us, he knows how much it can hurt. He knows how much he's asking. As you follow him, he certainly tests you and calls on you to sacrifice. Jesus said it: "Whoever wants to be my disciple must deny themselves and take up their cross and follow me" (Matthew 16:24). Sometimes it hurts more than we expect. Sometimes we wonder if God knows or cares how much it hurts.

There's a reason God called Abraham to sacrifice his son. We'll see that in our next devotion. But if you're struggling with the pain that comes with sacrifice or you wonder how a loving God could tell Abraham to sacrifice his son, consider this: The God who calls you to sacrifice knows exactly how much it hurts. After all, he sacrificed his Son—his only Son, Jesus, whom he loves—just for you. No matter how much he calls you to give, he's given even more in love for you.

Prayer: Heavenly Father, you've called me to take up my cross and follow Christ. Sometimes it feels as if you're asking too much, and I wonder if you understand just how much it hurts.

Hold Jesus' cross before my eyes so that I remember your love: You gave up your only Son for me. Even if I don't yet understand every reason for the sacrifices I need to make, help me to trust your love for me. Amen.

J.C.S.

For further reading, see The People's Bible commentary on Genesis, pages 176-184.

Confident Faith, Even in a Crisis of Faith

Bible Reading: Genesis 22:3-19

[Abraham] said to his servants, "Stay here with the donkey while I and the boy go over there. We will worship and then we will come back to you." (Genesis 22:5)

When God calls us to a life of faith, he gives us more than we can imagine, even though we can't grasp it at the time.

As much as believers have been offended at God calling Abraham to sacrifice Isaac, they've been even more amazed that Abraham was willing to do it. How could Abraham do such a thing? The New Testament book of Hebrews tells us what Abraham was thinking. God had promised Abraham that his descendants would be born through Isaac, but Isaac was still just a boy. Abraham understood that when God makes a promise, God keeps his promise. So he reasoned that if God was telling him to kill Isaac, then God would just have to raise Isaac back to life again (see Hebrews 11:17-19). He knew that God's command would end well, even if it meant going through incredible pain along the way. So as Abraham began his journey up the mountain with his only son—and the knife he intended to use to kill him—he confidently told his servants, "We will come back to you." God will keep his promise!

We know the ending of our story. We will stand with Christ, enjoying eternal life in heaven. And Jesus warns us that along the way we'll live as strangers in this world, we'll have trouble, and we'll pass through many hardships. So we prepare ourselves for the pain. And we know that sometimes the pain will be so severe that we'll have crises of faith. It will feel as though God is our enemy. It will feel as though God is there only to take away from us.

But God wanted Abraham to learn something. Abraham always knew he could trust in God. But as he prepared to slaughter his own son with the knife in his own hand and an angel from heaven called for him to stop, Abraham learned in an entirely new way that God isn't there to take from us. He's always there to give. How Abraham must have marveled at God's goodness as he hugged Isaac in his arms!

No matter how strong your faith is, you'll face crises at times. Do what Abraham did. Remind yourself that no matter how it seems, God will never lie. And even in a crisis of faith, say with a confident faith, "God will keep his promise!"

Prayer: Dear Savior, we know that it isn't a loss to follow you. We're willing to suffer rejection, loss, pain, and death because we know your love and the heaven that awaits us. Help us always see that even when you call us to sacrifice, it is never because you want to take from us. It is to show us that you will bless us more than we could ever expect. Amen.

J.C.S.

For further reading, see The People's Bible commentary on Genesis, pages 182-187.

Just a Piece of the Promise

Bible Reading: Genesis chapter 23

Then Abraham rose from beside his dead wife and spoke to the Hittites. He said, [4]"I am a foreigner and stranger among you. Sell me some property for a burial site here so I can bury my dead." (Genesis 23:3-4)

It's good to reflect on what God has promised us. He has promised us perfect peace with him. He has promised us victory over sin. He has promised us life in heaven. Now take stock of your life. Do you always feel perfect peace? Do you win every battle against sin? Are you standing on the glassy streets of heavenly gold?

If you ever get discouraged by the lack of these things, it's helpful to consider God's promises to Abraham. Abraham left his home and his father's family because the Lord had promised to give him a country of his own—a land flowing with milk and honey. The Lord had promised to make him into a great nation with descendants as numerous as the stars in the sky and to bless all peoples through him. Now, near the end of his life, Abraham had only two children (and only one through his wife, Sarah). He was no great blessing to the world yet. And when his wife Sarah died, he didn't own the land he was living in. He had to buy a little plot of land with a cave so he could bury his wife. Was it everything that God had promised him? No, not yet. But it was a piece of what was promised.

Or maybe we'd do better to call it a down payment. The author to the Hebrews acknowledges that Abraham—and every believer—lived and died without receiving the fullness of God's promises while here on earth. We just see the promised things and welcome them "from a distance" (Hebrews 11:13). The field Abraham bought to bury his wife wasn't much, but he realized what it was—just the first part of God's promise that would one day be fulfilled.

You have that too. God calls his Holy Spirit who lives in you as a "deposit," a down payment placed directly into your heart, guaranteeing you the rest of the blessings he'll give you (Ephesians 1:13-14). We still wrestle with worry, and we struggle against temptation. We don't stand in heaven yet. But let the faith you have, the hope and the joy that God gives you, be your own little "caves of Machpelah." They're your piece of God's promise, a down payment on what's to come.

Prayer: Gracious Lord, thank you for the Spirit's work in me. Through it, give me confidence that all your other promises to me will come true too. Amen.

J.C.S.

For further reading, see The People's Bible commentary on Genesis, pages 188-193.

God's Providence Serves His Promise

Bible Reading: Genesis chapter 24

"The Lord, the God of heaven, who brought me out of my father's household and my native land and who spoke to me and promised me on oath, saying, 'To your offspring I will give this land'—he will send his angel before you so that you can get a wife for my son from there." (Genesis 24:7)

Sarah's body already lay in the cave. At 140 years old, Abraham knew he would soon join her. But even when Abraham's body returned to dust, God would remember his promises to him. "Through your offspring all nations on earth will be blessed"

(Genesis 22:18). "It is through Isaac that your offspring will be reckoned" (Genesis 21:12).

It was time to find Isaac a wife. Many ancient customs sound strange to modern ears. Abraham would do the picking. Sort of. He would send his servant. But really the choice was God's.

Abraham's servant was loyal, but he still had questions. Abraham was sending the servant to his relatives 500 miles north. What if the woman he found was unwilling to leave her father and mother? Abraham knew the feeling. God had called him to do the same thing so many years ago. He knew it was a lot to ask.

But he also knew what God could do. The Lord and God who called him had kept his promise to bless him and give him a son. With confidence, Abraham assures his servant: "He will send his angel before you." Abraham's servant wasn't going alone on this mission.

Isn't it obvious? The events in the town of Nahor unfolded according to Abraham's expectations and his servant's prayer. God was behind the scenes, but just barely behind them. You can see his hands at work: Rebekah was willing to go without delay.

The work of God and the actions of Abraham create a beautiful harmony. God had made the promises. But that didn't mean Abraham sat on his hands. God's promises informed Abraham's actions. Then Abraham trusted God to bless.

God is always behind the scenes in your life too, even when it isn't so obvious. There's no need to worry. But don't sit on your hands either. Listen to his promises. Obey his will. Watch him honor your obedience by using it for his purposes. Even when your time on this earth is over, he'll continue to make it bear fruit.

Prayer: "As I pray, dear Jesus, hear me; let your words in me take root. May your Spirit e'er be near me that I bear abundant fruit. May I daily sing your praise, from my heart glad anthems raise, till my highest praise is given in the endless joy of heaven" (CW 631:4). Amen.

M.J.S.

For further reading, see The People's Bible commentary on Genesis, pages 193-204.

The Pain, Joy, and Blessing of Family

Bible Reading: Genesis chapter 25

Isaac prayed to the LORD on behalf of his wife, because she was childless. The LORD answered his prayer, and his wife Rebekah became pregnant. (Genesis 25:21)

The Lord had promised Eve that great pain would accompany the blessing of having children. But many women have also felt great pain from *not* having children. Sarah had felt it. Now Rebekah did too. Twenty years had passed since Isaac first brought her into his tent. The second generation of God's "great nation" was, yet again, without any children. In the town of Nahor, God had made it obvious that Rebekah was his choice for Isaac. Why did it have to be so hard to build a family?

In our day, both science and social services provide an array of options. Isaac's only hope was the only one whose help matters. He prayed to the Lord on behalf of his wife. How long he waited, we don't know. But, in his time, God answered doubly. There were two babies in Rebekah's womb. Soon they caused Rebekah a different kind of pain. They were fighting already *in utero*. She knew something wasn't right. When she inquired of the Lord, he prepared her for a prolonged struggle between the two—and their descendants. It would get worse.

Family was the first blessing. On the day God created Adam and Eve, he united them as one. He blessed them and said, "Be fruitful" (Genesis 1:28). And family is still a blessing—even though Satan and selfishness war against it. In one moment family is the greatest joy; in another it is the sharpest pain. Abraham and Sarah knew how far the pendulum could swing. For Isaac and Rebekah, this journey was just beginning. It would be a rough road. Not only would they suffer the pain, but they would cause their fair share of it too. But God would still bless their family and, as he had promised Abraham, make it a blessing (Genesis 22:18).

This is good for us to remember when our homes are hurting. When we're wondering why it has to be so hard, God can still bless. And he will—sometimes through the pain, sometimes in spite of the pain, and sometimes by relieving the pain—but always because of his love in Christ, by which he has made us members of his family. He's a perfect Father, and the only one whose help matters. "Isaac prayed to the LORD . . . the LORD answered his prayer."

Prayer: Father in heaven, I pray on behalf of everyone in my family: Heal and strengthen my home. Forgive my sins and give me a forgiving heart. Give me strength to address my messes in a way that pleases you. Fill me with grace, patience, and self-sacrificing love. Let your blessing fall on my family, and let my family bring honor to you. Amen.

M.J.S.

For further reading, see The People's Bible commentary on Genesis, pages 204-215.

Like Father, Like Son

Bible Reading: Genesis chapter 26

When the men of that place asked [Isaac] about his wife, he said, "She is my sister," because he was afraid to say, "She is my wife." He thought, "The men of this place might kill me on account of Rebekah, because she is beautiful." (Genesis 26:7)

Wait, what chapter is this? It sounds so familiar. Wasn't it Abraham who lied about his wife? He said Sarah was his sister because he was afraid that her beauty would get him killed—twice! The first time was in Egypt (Genesis 12). The second time was in Gerar (Genesis 20).

Now, at least 75 years after Abraham's lies in Gerar, his son was following in his footsteps. "Only the names have changed," we might want to say. But even many of the names were the same. Abimelek was a common name for Philistine kings, much like Henry and George in England. Phicol, the commander of his forces, also bore the same name as his predecessor in Abraham's day.

Like father, like son. Abraham had a sinful weakness, and he passed it on to Isaac. It was more than disregard for the truth. It was disregard for their wives. They were willing to preserve their safety by sacrificing their wives' chastity.

Kids are like sponges. We see it in Genesis. We can see it in the mirror. And if God has given you children, you can see it in them too. The Lord's words from Mt. Sinai should ring in our ears: "Punishing the children for the sin of the parents to the third and fourth generation of those who hate me" (Exodus 20:5). Why does he punish the children? Because they continue in the sins of the parents.

But there's something else that parents can give their children too. It doesn't come naturally like the passing of sin to the next generation. It takes work—lots of it. It requires love—lots of it. It's grace, and it's always greater than the sin of every generation because it was earned by the One who paid for the sins of the world on a cross. Where sin increased, grace increased all the more.

Isaac soaked up his father's sin like a sponge. But Abraham also passed on a promise to him. God made that promise take root and grow. If God has blessed you with children, remember that they are sponges. Put in the work. Pour out the love. Pass on the promise. It's not too late. Trust that God can make his promise take root and grow, just as he did in you.

Prayer: Dear Jesus, parents pass on their sin to their children, but they cannot take it away. Only you can take it away. Give parents love and patience to pass on your promise to their children so that your forgiveness may take root, down through the generations. Amen.

M.J.S.

For further reading, see The People's Bible commentary on Genesis, pages 215-223.

The Only Hope for a Broken Home Is Love

Bible Reading: Genesis chapter 27

Esau held a grudge against Jacob because of the blessing his father had given him. He said to himself, "The days of mourning for my father are near; then I will kill my brother Jacob." (Genesis 27:41)

If only Isaac, Rebekah, Esau, and Jacob had known that their family drama would be recorded for posterity! Would they have acted otherwise?

Everything is dysfunctional. Dad has his favorite. Mom has hers. Esau is rash. Jacob is deceitful—especially at his mother's urging. They're living proof of Jesus' words: "If a house is divided against itself, that house cannot stand" (Mark 3:25). By the end of the episode, Esau is plotting Jacob's murder and Rebekah is shipping Jacob hundreds of miles away under the pretense of finding a wife. Their duplicity leaves scars that will never fully heal.

This is the kind of thing that happens when families trade in love for self-interest and prefer to trust in their own machinations instead of the promises of God. Already when they were in her womb, the Lord had told Rebekah that "the older will serve the younger" (Genesis 25:23). But still, Isaac seems intent to give primacy to Esau, and Rebekah doesn't think twice about stooping low to stop him. When it's everyone for themselves, everyone gets hurt.

Would they have trusted more and deceived less if they had known people would still be reading their story four thousand years later? Not a chance. Reliance on the promises of God isn't produced by embarrassment. Fear of exposure will never cure self-interest. Love is the only cure. And it has to come from the outside. It has to come from God.

And he's got plenty to give. Even if it feels as if your home has been sucked so dry of love that the house itself makes you shiver, the love of God can restore warmth and life. Pray for him to start with you—no finger-pointing and no excuses. Only, "I have sinned." God responds with love: "I died to forgive you. That's right, I gave you myself. Even when all you could offer me was sin." His forgiveness warms your heart and gives you love to spare. That's the only way it works. He fills your heart with more than enough. Then it spills over onto the people closest to you. We love because he first loved us.

That's where it has to start—from the outside. Pray that God starts with you. When his love fills your heart, it will spill over into your home.

Prayer: Lord Jesus, when we were still sinners, you died for us. Fill me with your love for those who have wronged me so that I may give of myself to restore broken relationships and bring glory to your name. Amen.

M.J.S.

For further reading, see The People's Bible commentary on Genesis, pages 223-232.

When You Need It Most and Expect It Least, the Lord Is There

Bible Reading: Genesis chapter 28

When Jacob awoke from his sleep, he thought, "Surely the LORD is in this place, and I was not aware of it." [17] **He was afraid and said, "How awesome is this place! This is none other than the house of God; this is the gate of heaven."**

[18] **Early the next morning Jacob took the stone he had placed under his head and set it up as a pillar and poured oil on top of it.** (Genesis 28:16-18)

It could well be that Jacob used a stone for a pillow that night, but translations that say he put the stone *under* his head are a tad interpretive. He put it somewhere close to his head, so it's equally plausible that Jacob was employing the stone for protection, not comfort. He was outside on the open road. He needed all the help he could get—and he wasn't expecting to get it from the man upstairs.

He was about three days into a three-month journey. It must have been sinking in: "I'm alone. And it's my own fault. I made a fool of my father. I cheated my brother. I took things into my own hands because I gave up on God." The sun went down on his nightmare. He grabbed a rock—there was nothing else to hold on to. He lay down, longing for a do-over, but he couldn't turn back the clock.

We know the feeling. We convince ourselves that we are invincible to sin's consequences. Then our sins catch up with us, and we see up close what sin can do.

Exhausted from the journey, Jacob drifted to sleep. This wasn't the dream he expected—not then, not there. He thought he was alone. But then he saw a stairway that led straight from him in his mess to the Lord in heaven. He saw angels going up the stairs to tell God what he needed and angels coming back down to deliver his needs. He was sure God wasn't there. But God showed him otherwise in his dream. Jacob had turned his back, but the Lord who was faithful to Jacob's father and grandfather did not turn his back or walk away. "I am with you and will watch over you wherever you go" (28:15).

Jacob woke up in amazement. It wasn't just that God had stayed by his side, even when Jacob had turned his back. It was what God promised from the top of that stairway: the same family blessing that Jacob had weaseled out of his father and stolen from his brother. Jacob had given up on God and had tried to take it himself. But, as it turned out, it wasn't his to take. It was God's to give. And even after all his shenanigans, God still gave it.

Dear Christian friend, Jesus paid for your sins. If you've painted yourself into a corner with your sin and you see no way out, Jesus still connects you to God and his blessing. When you need it most and expect it least, the Lord is there to bless you.

Even when the road ahead is dark and rough, the Lord is there to bless you.

Prayer: Dear Lord, you promise to watch over my coming and going both now and forevermore (Psalm 121:8). Let that be my comfort and my confidence. Amen.

M.J.S.

For further reading, see The People's Bible commentary on Genesis, pages 232-238.

Jacob Meets His Match

Bible Reading: Genesis 29:1-30

When morning came, there was Leah! So Jacob said to Laban, "What is this you have done to me? I served you for Rachel, didn't I? Why have you deceived me?" (Genesis 29:25)

It's a textbook case of tasting your own medicine. Jacob had fled the aftermath of his deception only to plunge headlong into Laban's deceit. He had dressed up like his older brother; now Leah wore the dress of her younger sister. Now Jacob knew how it felt.

Laban was a master of his craft. By offering Jacob wages for his work, he subjected his own flesh and blood to servitude. When Jacob offered seven years of labor for Rachel's hand in marriage, Laban left loopholes in his response—he never explicitly agreed to give him Rachel! On the big day, he softened Jacob's senses with feasting and waited until dark to bring in the bride. He hid behind local customs to justify the ruse and squeezed another seven years of labor out of Jacob in the process.

Was it worth it, Laban? He subjected his daughters to lifelong rivalry in marriages that mocked God's design and promoted resentment and insecurity. Both daughters got the short end of the stick. Leah daily felt the sting of Jacob's love for Rachel. Rachel stewed in her own infertility.

Was it worth it? Jacob might have asked himself the same question. It was his own deceit that had sent him running to Laban. He had looked for refuge; he met his match.

But the Lord had made him a promise from the top of the stairway: "I am with you and will watch over you wherever you go" (Genesis 28:15). Jacob had made his bed. Now he was lying in it—but not alone. The Lord was watching over him even when the road was dark and rough. The Lord was training him. He was recasting him from a con artist into someone who would hold God to his promises. Jacob would be slow to learn. His story certainly highlights God's patience more than it highlights Jacob's path to spiritual maturity. But a promise is a promise. The Lord isn't a con man like Jacob and Laban. He doesn't look for loopholes in his words or ways to take advantage of his sons and daughters.

Even when we're lying in the bed of our own making and tasting our own medicine and the road is rough and dark, the Lord is true to his Word: "I am with you and will watch over you wherever you go." You can trust him.

Prayer: Lord, even when my sin is great, your grace is greater. Even when my path is dark, the light of your Word pierces the darkness. Teach me to trust your promises and to glorify you through my conduct. Amen.

M.J.S.

For further reading, see The People's Bible commentary on Genesis, pages 238-244.

Jesus' Broken Family

Bible Reading: Genesis 29:1–30:24

When Rachel saw that she was not bearing Jacob any children, she became jealous of her sister. So she said to Jacob, "Give me children, or I'll die!" (Genesis 30:1)

On the sixth day of creation God said, "It is not good for the man to be alone" (Genesis 2:18). But his design for marriage was one wife, not two. Jacob's family is Exhibit A for what happens when God's design is mocked.

To be fruitful and increase in number was a blessing from the Creator (Genesis 1:28). Leah and Rachel perverted it into a no-holds-barred competition. There were no winners.

For Leah, children were objects to win her husband's love. She freely admitted it. At Reuben's birth she said: "Surely my husband will love me now" (29:32). At Levi's: "At last my husband will become attached to me" (29:34). At Zebulun's: "This time my husband will treat me with honor" (30:20).

It was not much different for Rachel. She was already her husband's obvious favorite, but she was still determined to triumph over her sister. She sent her servant Bilhah into her husband's bed and chalked it up as a victory when Naphtali was born: "I have had a great struggle with my sister, and I have won" (30:8).

But we know the actual outcome when God's design for marriage is mocked—even perhaps from our own bitter experience. Everyone loses. Jacob's home was not a happy home.

There is nothing here to commend except the determined grace of God. "Through your offspring all nations on earth will be blessed," he had promised Abraham (Genesis 22:18). These were Abraham's offspring. The children of Israel. The nation from which the great serpent-crusher would come. From its very conception, this nation was Exhibit A of the determined grace of God.

This was Jesus' family. The people of Israel certainly didn't earn the honor. They demonstrated the need. They proved that salvation must be God's work. What he can do, even for broken families like this! What he can do, even from a broken family like this! They were his chosen people in spite of their sin, because of his Son.

Prayer: Merciful Father, you created family to be a blessing. You still bring blessing to broken families, and from them too. Send your Spirit to the homes of hurting families. Teach us how to forgive and love as you forgive and love us. Amen.

M.J.S.

For further reading, see The People's Bible commentary on Genesis, pages 238-251.

Reconciliation Is Better Than a Ceasefire

Bible Reading: Genesis 30:25–31:55

"This heap is a witness, and this pillar is a witness, that I will not go past this heap to your side to harm you and that you will not go past this heap and pillar to my side to harm me." (Genesis 31:52)

When Laban first met Jacob, he honored Jacob as a guest in his home. "You are my own flesh and blood," he told Jacob (Genesis 29:14). These two men had never met, but they shared a bond. They were family.

Now, after 20 years of deception, their bond was broken beyond repair. They entered into a covenant with a pile of stones as a witness. This wasn't an alliance. It was a ceasefire: Laban agreed to stay on his side of the line; Jacob agreed to stay on his.

Who bore the blame for this train wreck? It was Laban who pulled the switcheroo at Jacob's wedding and kept trying to squeeze more out of him at every turn. But Jacob wasn't an exemplar of honesty and selflessness either. He manipulated the mating of the flocks for his advantage; he conspired to flee while Laban's back was turned. There was a pattern here: First, Jacob's dishonesty in Canaan had forced him to flee to Aram. Now his dishonesty in Aram forced him to flee to Canaan.

So who bears the blame? That's often what we want to determine when a family comes unglued. We want to get to the bottom of it, determine who's in the right and who's in the wrong so we know whose side to take—or, when it's our own family, know how to persuade others to our side. But in most cases, it's not so simple. Both sides bear blame. It's as if everyone's sins have been thrown into a blender and mixed into a hot mess. There was a lot of finger-pointing going on between Jacob and Laban, but confession and forgiveness were nowhere to be found. And so, absent confession and forgiveness, the only workable solution was a ceasefire between enemies: "I'll stay on my side of the line as long as you stay on yours."

But there's something better than a ceasefire: reconciliation. Broken relationships can be restored in Jesus. Since "God was reconciling the world to himself in Christ, not counting people's sins against them" (2 Corinthians 5:19), we can be bold to confess our own sins instead of excusing them and to forgive others' sins instead of leveraging them.

The blood of Jesus doesn't stop at reconciling us to God. It has the power to restore our relationships with one another. It can heal even the deepest wounds.

Confess. Forgive. Don't be afraid to go first.

Prayer: Dear Lord Jesus, thank you for forgiving my sin and reconciling me to God. Fill me with your Spirit so that I may confess my sins to those I have sinned against and so that I may forgive those who have sinned against me. Amen.

M.J.S.

For further reading, see The People's Bible commentary on Genesis, pages 251-264.

The God Who Lets You Hold On to Him

Bible Reading: Genesis chapters 32 and 33

Then the man said, "Let me go, for it is daybreak." But Jacob replied, "I will not let you go unless you bless me." (Genesis 32:26)

The chickens were coming home to roost. Jacob was running out of places to hide. Leaving Laban meant facing Esau. Twenty years had passed since Jacob ran for his life from his brother, but time doesn't necessarily heal all wounds. Afraid of what would come from this mess he'd made, Jacob split his caravan into two groups to mitigate losses in case of an attack. He prayed for God to remain faithful to the promise. He sent gifts ahead in droves in hopes of softening Esau before their reunion. He did what he could, but some troubles seemed too deep to ever overcome.

Maybe you've been in a place like that. You figured you could take care of yourself just fine—even though your gain came at the expense of others. But then you messed everything up so bad that you had nowhere else to turn. So you pleaded in prayer: "Lord, save me!" And then all you could do was wait.

While Jacob waited, it only got worse. A stranger attacked. Somewhere along the line, Jacob realized that his adversary was

God. But instead of letting go or running away, he held on even tighter: "I will not let you go unless you bless me."

It's tempting to see Jacob as the hero of this episode: He held on to God—even when God appeared to be the enemy!

But even more amazing was that God let Jacob hold on to him. Even after more than 20 years of Jacob's deception and thievery, God hadn't given up on him. He refused to rescind his promise. He continued to teach Jacob that he could trust him, even when he appeared to be the enemy.

If you look in the mirror and see someone not so different from Jacob, if you look at your circumstances and are tempted to wonder whose side God is on, then take another look at God's promise of your forgiveness in Jesus. Remember the claim God made on you at your baptism. He's the hero of your story. Grab on to him and refuse to let go.

Prayer: Heavenly Father, my sins are many. The damage they have caused is great. But on the cross Jesus paid for the sins of the world—even mine. You declared me your child at my baptism. Teach me to hold on to you in faith and to never let go, no matter what I see or how I feel. Amen.

M.J.S.

For further reading, see The People's Bible commentary on Genesis, pages 264-278.

Sin Snowballs

Bible Reading: Genesis chapter 34

When Shechem son of Hamor the Hivite, the ruler of that area, saw [Dinah], he took her and raped her. (Genesis 34:2)

The sons of Jacob came upon the dead bodies and looted the city where their sister had been defiled. (Genesis 34:27)

A snowball that fits in someone's hand at the top of a mountain can grow into an avalanche by the time it reaches the bottom. It picks up so much mass and speed that nothing can stop it from wiping out a village.

That's the way sin works too. A young man with a powerful father lusted after Jacob's daughter, Dinah. But his lust wasn't content to stay in the confines of his heart. This snowball grew into rape. Even then, his lust refused to be satisfied.

If it stopped there, it would be tragedy enough. But it kept rolling and pulled others in. Dinah's brothers were right to be furious, but in their anger, they fought sin with more sin. They weaponized God's covenant of circumcision. Simeon and Levi turned a village into a bloodbath, and their brothers peeled plunder from the corpses.

When our fallen natures take the lead in addressing sin, it only makes things worse. When *he-hit-me* justifies *I-hit-him-back,* the result is mutual destruction. From playgrounds to marriages, we see it everywhere. We see it in ourselves.

In our corrupted world, God has appointed authorities to use force to keep wickedness in check. But the rule of law and the retaliation of the justice system are Band-Aids. They cannot cure the disease.

Only forgiveness can stop the cycle. And forgiveness comes only from Jesus. He is God, which means every sin is a crime against him. But he so loved the offenders that he called every sin his own. He paid the price that we all owed him. By his wounds we are healed.

Only forgiveness can stop the cycle. And forgiveness comes only from Jesus. But one way that he gives forgiveness is through you. A forgiven Christian is a forgiving Christian. When you or people you love are wronged, you're not left to perpetuate the cycle and make the avalanche even worse. "Love covers over a multitude of sins" (1 Peter 4:8).

Prayer: Dear Jesus, when you were insulted, you did not retaliate; when you suffered, you made no threats. Instead, you entrusted yourself to him who judges justly (1 Peter 2:23). Grant that I forgive those who have wronged me and that I show compassion and mercy to all who have been wronged. Amen.

M.J.S.

For further reading, see The People's Bible commentary on Genesis, pages 278-286.

Jacob's Pillar

Bible Reading: Genesis chapters 35 and 36

Then God said to Jacob, "Go up to Bethel and settle there, and build an altar there to God, who appeared to you when you were fleeing from your brother Esau." (Genesis 35:1)

About 30 years had passed since Jacob fled his father's house. In his effort to improve his own position, he had lost everything—almost everything. A few days into his journey, God had appeared to him at Bethel and showed him otherwise: "I am with you and will watch over you wherever you go, and I will bring you back to this land. I will not leave you until I have done what I have promised you" (Genesis 28:15). Even when Jacob needed it most and expected it least, the Lord was there to bless him. Jacob had set up a stone at Bethel as a pillar and had made a vow: If God would bring him back safely, Jacob would worship God at this place.

God kept his promise, but Jacob was slow in keeping his. Years after returning to the land, God prompted Jacob to return to Bethel. It was a wake-up call for Jacob. For decades God had been training Jacob to trust in him, but Jacob was slow to learn.

He disposed of the foreign gods that had accumulated in his household and returned to Bethel. God's intention there wasn't to squeeze anything out of Jacob. It was to fill him up. God repeated the promise he had made so many years earlier, the same promise he had made to Abraham and Isaac. Jacob's backsliding would not make a liar of God. And God, in grace, kept pulling Jacob back to his promise.

It didn't mean Jacob's life would be easy. He was familiar with loss and pain. Some of it was the direct result of a specific sin. Some was simply the general result of living in a sinful world. All of it taught him to rely on the one reliable pillar in his life, the one faithful constant. Even when he lost the love of his life, even when his eldest son committed unspeakable betrayal, even when burying his father required facing his estranged brother, even when he needed it most and expected it least and didn't deserve it at all, the Lord was there to bless him. The Lord was his pillar.

Prayer: Lord God, my faithfulness to you has been fickle, but your faithfulness to me never fails. Thank you for drawing me back to your promises today. Strengthen me through them. Amen.

M.J.S.

For further reading, see The People's Bible commentary on Genesis, pages 286-299.

When Love Isn't Love

Bible Reading: Genesis chapter 37

Now Israel loved Joseph more than any of his other sons, because he had been born to him in his old age; and he made an ornate robe for him. (Genesis 37:3)

There were reasons why Joseph was Jacob's favorite son. Joseph was the miracle baby that Jacob (Israel's other name) had in his old age. Joseph wasn't his firstborn; Jacob had ten other sons through three other women by the time he held Joseph in his arms. But Joseph was the son of the one woman he'd loved more than all the rest, the one who'd been denied a child for so long.

And what a son he was! Joseph seemed to excel at everything Jacob gave to him, and Jacob gave him a lot. He eventually gave Joseph a role of watching over his older brothers, reporting back to Jacob on how they did. It was an impressive job, and Jacob gave Joseph an impressive robe to match. Jacob poured out love on Joseph. . . . So Jacob likely told himself.

The love we show rarely comes without sin and selfishness attached. Jacob loved Joseph because he was born to him in his old age, because he was born of the wife Jacob loved most of all, and because Joseph was gifted.

Jacob's life teaches us the danger of playing favorites with our love. It's no different than when a mother today dotes upon her perfect son but keeps her troubled daughter at arm's length or when a pastor is quick to visit the church president after his surgery but never makes it out to the delinquent who seems to have nothing to offer but excuses and empty promises. Playing favorites shows how broken our sense of love really is. When we play favorites, we're really not loving someone else; we're just loving ourselves. Just ask Joseph, who paid the price for his father's "love" as his own brothers sold him into slavery.

But there's another lesson from Jacob's life. His sense of love was self-centered and broken, but God's isn't. It took years to see it and cost tears to get there, but God used Jacob's self-centered love to bring blessings to so many people through Joseph. He raised Joseph to authority and power. He used Joseph to save his brothers' lives. He used him to bless the pagan nation of Egypt. He even used him to bring joy and deliverance to Jacob, the father whose sin started all of this. God is that kind of Father. He doesn't play favorites. He loves all his children.

Prayer: Thank you, Father, for your undeserved love for a sinful child like me. Help me to love everyone in my life just as you have loved me. Amen.

J.C.S.

For further reading, see The People's Bible commentary on Genesis, pages 300-309.

Inescapable Shame

Bible Reading: Genesis chapter 38

As [Tamar, Judah's daughter-in-law] was being brought out, she sent a message to her father-in-law. "I am pregnant by the man who owns these," she said. And she added, "See if you recognize whose seal and cord and staff these are."

26 Judah recognized them and said, "She is more righteous than I, since I wouldn't give her to my son Shelah." And he did not sleep with her again. (Genesis 38:25-26)

I overheard a coffee shop conversation years ago that has stayed with me. A small group had met for Bible study and discussion over coffee when a member asked, "Should parents ever apologize to their children?" For the next 15 minutes, the group agonized over the question, exploring the pros and cons as to whether or not parents should admit they were wrong to their children.

Judah didn't have the luxury of agonizing over this answer. The history and customs seem strange to us, but the sin was clear enough. Judah's firstborn son, Er, married a woman named Tamar. But Er was wicked, and the Lord put him to death. The custom in the land was to provide for a grieving widow by giving her in marriage to the next eldest brother, so Tamar married Onan. Onan was wicked too, and the Lord put him to death also. With two sons in the ground, Judah did not want to risk his third son. It was much easier to let the burden fall on Tamar, his daughter-in-law. *Better a poor and lonely widow than another dead son*, he thought.

Tamar likely wasn't occupying Judah's thoughts years later when he decided to sleep with a prostitute he met on the side of the road. If she had been on his mind, he might have recognized that he wasn't propositioning a prostitute but his own disguised daughter-in-law! The support Judah hadn't given to Tamar willingly she would get through deceit. Three months later, with his own sin far from memory, when Judah heard that his widowed and unwed daughter-in-law was pregnant, he was ready to call for her death as punishment for sin. His "righteous anger" faded when she produced evidence. Yes, she was an unwed mother, but he himself was the father. Ashamed, he admitted his guilt.

The history and customs seem strange, but the truth isn't. What do children learn from their parents? We don't just pass on lessons in tying shoes and reciting ABCs. Children learn about sin from us too. They don't just hear about it in Bible readings; they see it in our actions and our failures.

So teach them something else too. Teach them confession as you admit your sins. Don't deceive yourself with the thought that you'll be able to sweep your sins under the rug. Show them what confession looks like and teach them the joy of knowing they're forgiven.

Prayer: Heavenly Father, keep us from the foolishness of hiding our sins while condemning the sins of others. Give us the wisdom to confess our sins and find joy in your forgiveness. Amen.

J.C.S.

For further reading, see The People's Bible commentary on Genesis, pages 309-318.

When No One Is Watching, God Is Still Loving

Bible Reading: Genesis chapter 39

"No one is greater in this house than I am. My master has withheld nothing from me except you, because you are his wife. How then could I do such a wicked thing and sin against God?" (Genesis 39:9)

It's hard to face life's challenges when you're not loved—when you're all alone.

Joseph was about 17 years old when he was sold into slavery. If anyone had asked him how he found himself in chains, he would have had to hang his head and answer, "My brothers sold me. This is how much my own flesh and blood hated me."

Joseph became a slave in the house of an Egyptian named Potiphar, the captain of Pharaoh's guard. By this time, he'd been enslaved for about three years. Three years of being away from the father he loved. Three years of bearing the shame of brothers who hated him. Three years of being a slave in a foreign land. So when a powerful and beautiful woman—Potiphar's wife!—tried to seduce a 20-year-old man who'd known so much rejection and hatred, well, who could resist such a tempting escape from loneliness? Especially when rejecting her advances could bring more hardship? Especially when he'd been so unloved?

Except Joseph wasn't unloved. Twice in the chapter God reminds us of a truth of Joseph's life: "The LORD was with him." Even though he was rejected and hated by his family, Joseph understood that there wasn't just a righteous God watching his every move; he had a loving Lord who would never leave him.

And he won't leave you, either. At your baptism, God adopted you as his child. Can you count the ways he tells you of his love? You can never flee from his presence (Psalm 139:7). He's inscribed your name on the palms of his hand (Isaiah 49:16). Never will he leave you or forsake you (Hebrews 13:5). He is "with you always, to the very end of the age" (Matthew 28:20). When you face temptations that seem too hard to face, remember those promises.

And on the days that you fall into sin, go back to those promises and remember that it's still true: The Lord is with you.

Prayer: Whatever my struggles, dear Lord, whatever temptations I will face today, remind me that I will never face them alone. Through your Word and sacraments, remind me that I am loved, forgiven, and never alone. And bless me as I live for you. Amen.

J.C.S.

For further reading, see The People's Bible commentary on Genesis, pages 318-324.

Serving in the Depths

Bible Reading: Genesis chapter 40

The chief cupbearer, however, did not remember Joseph; he forgot him. (Genesis 40:23)

He was far from the home of his loving father. His own brothers had betrayed him. Then he learned the pain of prison, chains, and punishment. He was in the depths.

Such was the life of Joseph. Or is that a description of Jesus instead? It's amazing how Joseph's life traces so many of the same outlines that Jesus would later complete.

Consider Joseph: The Lord put him in the depths. The man who was sold into slavery by his brothers and wrongly imprisoned by his master finds himself jailed with two other men. The pharaoh of Egypt had locked up his baker and cupbearer in the same prison as Joseph and had forgotten about them. But God hadn't forgotten Joseph. So when those two prisoners shared that they both had mysterious dreams the previous night but had no idea what they meant, what did Joseph do? He interpreted them by God's power. The dreams meant death for one man and life for the other. Joseph served, there in the depths where God had placed him. He served, knowing that even in the depths he was carrying out God's will.

Nearly two thousand years later, Jesus wasn't imprisoned with two men; he was crucified with them. One was lost in his own hatred and bound for destruction. The other? Jesus spoke the words of forgiveness and life he needed to hear. Jesus served, there in the depths where God had placed him.

Sometimes God puts us in low places. But it's never because he's abandoned us or turned his love away from us. Even in the depths, he has us right where he wants us. He puts us in the depths so we can serve others there with his love. And he might leave us there for a while—Joseph was forgotten in prison for two more years—but just as he raised up Jesus from the dead, so too he'll remember his love for us.

Until that day, let your life follow the outlines and patterns of Jesus' life and of Joseph's life. You know that God will raise you to the heights. Don't be afraid to show that love in the depths. If God put you there, that's where he'll use you.

Prayer: I am confident of your love that will bring me home to heaven, Lord. Give me courage and love to serve wherever you've placed me today. Amen.

J.C.S.

For further reading, see The People's Bible commentary on Genesis, pages 324-328.

All in God's Time

Bible Reading: Genesis chapter 41

> **"The reason the dream was given to Pharaoh in two forms is that the matter has been firmly decided by God, and God will do it soon."** (Genesis 41:32)

The entire story of Joseph's life fills 14 chapters in Genesis. That's almost one-third of the book, but it doesn't take a lot of time to read. It's easy to miss how many years went by. In chapter 37, Joseph was sold into slavery by his brothers when he was about 17 years old. By the time he's elevated to the second highest position in Egypt at the end of chapter 41, he's 30. Those five chapters cover 13 years of suffering, hardship, and disappointment.

It's hard not to wonder if there was any bitterness in Joseph's words to Pharaoh. Pharaoh had called Joseph out of prison to interpret two troubling dreams that the leader had had the night before. Joseph shared that the reason God gave Pharaoh the dreams in two forms was because "God will do it soon."

This wasn't the first time God had given a message in the form of two dreams. When Joseph was a young man, the Lord had given him two dreams showing that he would be raised up to a position of glory and authority. Of course, now those dreams were 13 years in the past.

"The matter has been firmly decided by God, and God will do it *soon.*" As Joseph said it, did he think of his two dreams from so long ago? Did Joseph wonder why God was taking so long to keep his promises to him?

Do you? God hasn't just made you a promise twice. He repeats promises of his love and his blessings for you throughout the pages of Scripture. He tells you that all things will work for your good. That he will provide all you need. That he will return and bring you home to heaven. Do you ever feel like Joseph, waiting for God to keep his promises?

God's *soon* isn't always the same as ours, but it's always true. For Joseph, God kept his promises in his good time. He will for you too, at the right time. After all, he's firmly decided it.

Prayer: Dear Lord, you are not slow in keeping your promises. In your patient love, you guide the days of our lives to accomplish salvation for us and for many others. Whatever my struggles may be today, give me trust in your love and your wisdom, knowing that you will grant me relief at just the right time. Amen.

J.C.S.

For further reading, see The People's Bible commentary on Genesis, pages 328-339.

Guilt Grows . . .

Bible Reading: Genesis chapters 42 and 43

[Joseph's brothers] said to one another, "Surely we are being punished because of our brother. We saw how distressed he was when he pleaded with us for his life, but we would not listen; that's why this distress has come on us." (Genesis 42:21)

God describes his Word as a seed. We plant it when we share his Word with others, and as God gives his blessing, the Word grows. But God's Word isn't the only thing we plant. We also plant guilt. And guilt can grow just as well.

As the years went on, maybe Joseph's brothers had begun to talk less about the day they had thought that selling their brother into slavery was a far more righteous path than actually killing him. They might have learned to bear the lines of sadness etched into their father Jacob's face and to ignore the way that laughter and joy had been drained from their childhood home. We can do that. We can tell ourselves that if the damages our sins have done aren't really all that bad, then our sins must not be that bad either. And for years, it can feel as though it's really true. But guilt doesn't go away. Quietly and slowly, beneath the surface, it grows.

Soon enough Joseph's brothers would find out that he was alive. But right now, there was nothing to remind them of their great sin from more than a decade ago—and they didn't need a reminder. It still weighed on their hearts. As soon as hardship struck them, their consciences sprang to life. They thought of their brother's screams for mercy falling on their deaf ears. "God must be punishing us for our sins!"

It might not seem like it, but that feeling of guilt was a blessing. It prepared them to confess their sins and find the forgiveness and healing God gives. That forgiveness is found in the next chapter. But for now, if you have felt the guilt of unaddressed sins from long ago weighing on you, understand that the solution isn't burying the guilt even deeper. It will just be all the more rooted in your life. Take heart that your conscience is still living and active, and know that God blesses you with a conscience for a reason.

Prayer: Lord, we ask for your healing, especially on long-harbored guilt, hidden in secret. Give us faith to confess that sin to you, knowing that your sacrifice on the cross has already paid for it in full. And give us strength, dear Lord, to confess our sins to others who still carry hurt or pain from our actions, that you might bring peace and healing to them. Amen.

J.C.S.

For further reading, see The People's Bible commentary on Genesis, pages 339-357.

. . . And Forgiveness Grows Too

Bible Reading: Genesis chapters 44 and 45

Then [Joseph] threw his arms around his brother Benjamin and wept, and Benjamin embraced him, weeping. 15 And he kissed all his brothers and wept over them. (Genesis 45:14-15)

When guilt for an unconfessed sin bothers us, we tell ourselves that we'll get used to it or the feeling will pass. But guilt is like any other burden: the longer you carry it, the heavier it gets. For two decades Joseph's brothers had held inside their guilt over betraying their brother. Can you imagine the feelings that must have haunted them every time they saw their father cry over his lost son?

Maybe you can. Maybe you know that feeling too. When you read through Genesis chapters 44–45, you can see what guilt like that does. You can get so used to the feelings of shame that it becomes impossible to think forgiveness can be real.

So God shows us something wonderful. No matter how enormous our guilt grows, forgiveness always grows bigger. If you doubt that, consider the news that Joseph's brothers received: Not only was Joseph alive, but God had used their sin of betraying him to save countless lives. Not only were they safe, but Joseph would bring their entire family to Egypt, take care of them, and bless them with the best of the land. Not only was the brother they betrayed second-in-command of Egypt, but he was using all his power to love and bless the people who had sought to kill him. Forgiveness like that seems impossible, but it's the gift God gives.

If there's someone against whom you're holding a grudge and you're sure they would never repent, consider this possibility: They may be holding on to more guilt and fear than you could ever imagine. It may be crushing their heart and killing their hope. Prepare your heart to forgive them in a way that shows God's love is greater than their guilt.

And if you've been hiding a sin in your heart and it feels too big, too shameful, or too destructive to ever confess, remember that God's love is greater than your guilt too. Your pain may have been growing, but confess that sin and see how God's forgiveness grows too.

Prayer: Dear Savior, give me courage and love to confess my hidden sins and to give grace and forgiveness to those who have hurt me. Amen.

J.C.S.

For further reading, see The People's Bible commentary on Genesis, pages 357-370.

Ready to Die

Bible Reading: Genesis chapters 46 and 47

Israel said to Joseph, "Now I am ready to die, since I have seen for myself that you are still alive." (Genesis 46:30)

Even when we have peace with God, it can be hard to die. We know that heaven is our home through faith in Christ, but other concerns weigh on us. Certainly our fears about physical pain trouble our minds. We might worry about how long we'll linger in poor health or even be concerned about the strength of our faith in our dying moments. But perhaps our greatest worry is simply this: Will the people I love be okay?

Jacob wasn't a man of weak faith. He'd wrestled with God—literally! The Lord had comforted him when he was running away from his problems and had promised him blessings time and again. Jacob knew God's grace and knew his heavenly home. He wasn't afraid to die, but he hadn't been ready yet either.

When Jacob saw his son Joseph more than 20 years after he was first told that Joseph had been killed, God gave Jacob a different kind of peace. If any part of his heart had held on to guilt about Joseph's "death," Jacob could finally let that go, seeing with his own eyes that God was using everything for Joseph's good—and not just for Joseph's good: Jacob's family had a new home. God would see them safely through this time of famine. God had brought peace between Joseph and his brothers. Jacob could die, confident that his loved ones were okay.

It's a special privilege to know that the people you love are going to be okay. Use your time in this life to pray for those you love, to provide for them, and to use your words and your example to be faithful to the Savior. And if God doesn't give you the blessing of seeing with your own eyes that your loved ones will be okay, as he did for Jacob, remember that your Savior committed his spirit to his Father in heaven and died at peace, knowing he paid for the sins of all people. You can entrust those you love to him and be ready to die at peace too.

Prayer: Heavenly Father, bless my efforts to provide for those I love, physically and spiritually. And when my last hour comes, help me remember that you love them too, so I can die at peace. Amen.

J.C.S.

For further reading, see The People's Bible commentary on Genesis, pages 370-384.

The Blessing Among the Blessings

Bible Reading: Genesis chapters 48 and 49

The scepter will not depart from Judah,
nor the ruler's staff from between his feet,
until he to whom it belongs shall come
and the obedience of the nations shall be his.
(Genesis 49:10)

"Genesis is the story of . . . "

How would you finish that sentence? Genesis lives up to the meaning of its Greek name: "the beginning." We've read about the beginning of the world, the origin of humans and sin and pain, and the first promises of a Savior.

Genesis is also the story of a family, with all its happiness and heartbreak. We've read about cowardly husbands who sought to save their own skin rather than show holy love for their wives, extended family members who tried to cheat their relatives at every turn, extramarital affairs, bloodshed, and brothers at each other's throats. And we've read of the joys of unexpected babies gracing couples' golden years and the blessing of long-harbored guilt forgiven and relationships restored. Genesis is the story of all that.

And more than any of that, Genesis is the story of Jesus. Nearing the book's close, Jacob spoke a final blessing to each of his sons—the men whose descendants would become the 12 tribes of Israel. And he made a strange promise to Judah. Even though Jacob's family was simply a gathering of 70 relatives and servants, he prophesied that Judah's clan would hold on to kingly power until the power would come to the descendant to whom it would truly belong—the one who would reign over the nations. It was a promise of Jesus. Jerusalem, Israel's capital, would be in Judah's tribal land, and Judah's descendants—such as King David—would sit on Israel's throne. Then, in the fullness of time, Jesus, descended from Judah, would come, and God would exalt him as our heavenly King.

All the joys and sadnesses, betrayals and reconciliations led to this promise. And God would use the next two thousand years of biblical history to bring that prophecy to fulfillment. It was all the story of Jesus. Cherish that truth of God's guiding hand in history—and take another look at your life. God's been working through it all to bring you to faith and keep you in his peace. Your story is the story of Jesus too.

Prayer: Lord of my life, you lead me through times of happiness and sadness, prosperity and loss, guilt and forgiveness. Help me to see my life as part of the story of Jesus, to see his love and your gracious plan throughout. Help me to treasure that as the greatest blessing you give, and use me to share that blessing with others. Amen.

J.C.S.

For further reading, see The People's Bible commentary on Genesis, pages 384-400.

How to Forgive

Bible Reading: Genesis chapter 50

Joseph said to them, "Don't be afraid. Am I in the place of God?" (Genesis 50:19)

Perhaps this is the hardest thing about forgiveness: It's unfair. We look at someone who has caused us lifelong hurt—sometimes simply out of sinful hatred or jealousy—and we forgive them. We tell them that not only are we letting go of our anger, but we'll actually show them kindness and love. We are repaying evil with good. We are loving those who hated us and helping those who harmed us.

Recall what Joseph's brothers had done to him: After planning to murder him, they instead sold him into slavery when he was only 17. They told his father the lie that he'd been killed. They stole from Joseph his freedom, his fatherland, and his family and doomed him to more than a decade of serving as a slave and a prisoner. It had now been almost 20 years since their first tearful reunion with Joseph, when he had explained that God had used their sin to accomplish boundless good and save countless lives. He'd relocated their families to Egypt and blessed them with the best of the land. But no matter how much Joseph assured them of forgiveness, their sins must have seemed like an impossible debt to cancel.

But we're not the ones who cancel it. Over the last three decades of his life, Joseph learned that no matter how much someone betrays us, the Lord is still with us. No matter how much people hurt us, God will use it for our good. As Joseph's brothers stood before him in guilt and fear, worrying that he was *finally* going to take his revenge, God taught us all through Joseph that it's not our job to settle scores. The Lord knows how to dispense justice. By not standing in God's place as judge, Joseph stood in God's place to forgive.

No doubt throughout your reading of Genesis you've seen a lot of your family life and your own personal failings on display. God grant that you see yourself in Joseph too. People's sins against you are real. They hurt, and they're hard to forgive. But you're not in God's place as their judge. May God help us see his faithful presence in our lives and help us see his ability to use all hurts for our good. And when we step out of God's role as judge, may he teach us to forgive as he does.

Prayer: Almighty God, wherever you've placed me in life, help me see the ways I may reflect your will and your love. Amen.

J.C.S.

For further reading, see The People's Bible commentary on Genesis, pages 400-406.

God Is Hands-On, Even in Hardship

Bible Reading: Exodus chapter 1

Then a new king, to whom Joseph meant nothing, came to power in Egypt. (Exodus 1:8)

Genesis ended like a fairy tale. Joseph had risen from dungeon to throne. Israel's broken family was reunited and reconciled. They could see God's fingerprints all over their happiness.

But already in the first verses of Exodus, the fairy tale gave way to a nightmare. Joseph and his brothers had long since passed from the scene. A new king had assumed the throne. He either didn't know about Joseph or didn't care about Egypt's arrangement with Joseph's family. The Israelites were a clear and present danger to the king. When enslaving them only served to strengthen them, he shifted his strategy to destroying them.

But do not assume that Pharaoh's tyranny and the Israelites' misery are evidence of a hands-off God. God hadn't forgotten.

In fact, he was setting the stage to put his power and faithful love on full display. He had made a promise to these enslaved people. He heard their groaning. He was about to show the world that he is a God who saves.

Exodus isn't an underdog story about the people on the ropes who bounce back to the top by their own tenacity and wit. Exodus is about God preserving the offspring of the woman, even as the offspring of the serpent wages war against them (Genesis 3:15). He had chosen the Israelites to be the people from whom the Savior would come to crush the serpent's head. Neither the serpent nor the pharaoh nor Moses' failings nor the Israelites' opposition to his gracious deliverance would stand in his way. God is the hero of this story. The glory is his alone.

Prayer: Dear Father, I trust your promise that you are in heaven, ruling over all things for the sake of your promises and your chosen ones. Help me see everything in the past, present, and future as the unfolding of your gracious will to save the world from sin and death. Use the hardships that overwhelm me to lift my eyes of faith to you, my only Savior. When I am weak, in you I am strong. Amen.

M.J.S.

For further reading, see The People's Bible commentary on Exodus, pages 8-13.

Nothing Is Random With God

Bible Reading: Exodus chapter 2

The Israelites groaned in their slavery and cried out, and their cry for help because of their slavery went up to God. [24] God heard their groaning and he remembered his covenant with Abraham, with Isaac and with Jacob. [25] So God looked on the Israelites and was concerned about them. (Exodus 2:23-25)

If you read them in isolation, the first 22 verses of Exodus chapter 2 appear to form a mountain of impossible coincidences.

The baby boy in the basket wound up in the hands of Pharaoh's daughter. Her father had ordered his people to throw Hebrew boys *into* the Nile River to kill them. She pulled the baby boy *out of* the river to spare his life. Eventually, he lived right under Pharaoh's nose. What a happy coincidence!

Baby Moses was returned to his own mother to be nursed. The royal house paid her to care for the person who would liberate its slaves and devastate its country. What a happy coincidence!

Moses was forced to flee far from Egypt on account of his ill-conceived attempt to rescue one of his own people. Even his own people turned on him for trying to help. Oh—that one isn't so happy. How could Moses help the people from exile in Midian?

But none of these events was random. The last verses of the chapter let us in on something that no one in Egypt or Midian could see: "God heard their groaning . . . he remembered his covenant . . . and was concerned." Expressions like this in the Old Testament always indicate that God was about to act. God never stopped hearing or remembering or being concerned.

When Moses' mother put the basket into the river and when Pharaoh's daughter drew him out, they had no idea of what God would do through this child. When Moses' act of murder forced him to flee Egypt, he had no idea of the mission for which God was preparing him. But God knew. Unbeknownst to anyone on earth, God was orchestrating these apparent coincidences to answer the prayers of his people, to fulfill his promises, and to save the world through his Son.

Prayer: Almighty God, no detail escapes your notice. No event lies outside your control. Even when your enemies rage against you and your people cry out in pain, you're at work and using it all to bring glory to your name and salvation to your chosen ones—even me. Thank you. Amen.

M.J.S.

For further reading, see The People's Bible commentary on Exodus, pages 13-20.

God Uses His People to Accomplish His Purpose

Bible Reading: Exodus 3:1-10

"So I have come down to rescue them from the hand of the Egyptians and to bring them up out of that land into a good and spacious land, a land flowing with milk and honey—the home of the Canaanites, Hittites, Amorites, Perizzites, Hivites and Jebusites." (Exodus 3:8)

"So now, go. I am sending you to Pharaoh to bring my people the Israelites out of Egypt." (Exodus 3:10)

At 80 years old, Moses' age had doubled since his exile began. Egypt was a memory. His life was in Midian now. And as he saw it, it was likely winding down. Eighty years was a full life.

He wasn't planning on an encounter with God. He could not have foreseen that in a year or so he'd be leading a nation of two million-plus people to this same mountain for their own encounter with God.

But then, while Moses' flocks nibbled at the desert scrub, something caught his eye—a burning bush. God's own voice called him by name. Moses was on holy ground. He was afraid, but the God of his fathers had good news. God had seen his people's misery. He had heard their cries. He was concerned. He came down to keep his promises to Abraham, Isaac, and Jacob. "I have come down to rescue them."

And how was God going to rescue them? He said to Moses, "So now, go. I am sending you."

If we were the authors of history, we'd likely have God do it himself. He could have just said the word and it all would have been done. Quick and easy. But that's not the way God generally works. He uses his people. We may feel too worn out, too inept. But God doesn't use us because we bring so much to the table. He uses us because that's what he created us for and that's what he redeemed us for—to be his voice, his hands, the agents of his love. God gives us the high privilege of joining him in his work, and he uses what we do in his name to accomplish his purpose.

Prayer: Dear Father, as your redeemed child, I am your handiwork, created in Christ Jesus to do good works. Regardless of my station in life, continue to fill me with your love and to equip me with everything I need to glorify you by serving others. Amen.

M.J.S.

For further reading, see The People's Bible commentary on Exodus, pages 20-23.

Who Am I?

Bible Reading: Exodus 3:11–4:17

Moses said to God, "Who am I that I should go to Pharaoh and bring the Israelites out of Egypt?"
12 And God said, "I will be with you." (Exodus 3:11-12)

God called Moses to the high privilege of joining him in his work. The Lord promised to use what Moses did in his name to accomplish his purpose.

But Moses didn't want to do it. Count his objections: Who am I? . . . Who are you? . . . What if they don't believe me? . . . I'm not eloquent. And finally, Please send someone else!

Before we stand in judgment, we should consider what Moses was up against: He knew the might of Pharaoh firsthand. The most powerful nation on earth considered Pharaoh a god. And then there were all the unknowns: After centuries of slavery, what if the Israelites no longer remembered the God of Abraham, Isaac, and Jacob? What if they didn't recognize Moses as God's prophet? What if Moses' speech wasn't up to par?

Before we stand in judgment, we should also consider our own reluctance and refusal to carry out the work that God has set before us. There are aspects of our personal callings that we carry out with joy. But there are also those things that require courage and sacrifice and that may result in rejection. Objections and excuses abound in our hearts: *I don't have gifts . . . or the time . . . or the emotional fortitude.* Instead of seeing the honor of joining God in his mission, we turn in on ourselves and wish the responsibility away: *Somebody else should do it.*

When Moses was turned in on himself and was pouring out excuses, "the LORD's anger burned against Moses" (Exodus 4:14). But notice what else God did. He refocused Moses on him—the sovereign, unchanging, faithful "I AM"—by saying, "I will be with you." Pharaoh was a god to the Egyptians, but Moses had the Lord on his side. The Lord would go with Moses, equip him, and send people to help him. This wasn't about what Moses could do for God but what God would do through Moses.

"If God himself be for me, I may a host defy" (CW 819:1).

Prayer: Dear Jesus, forgive my resentment and reluctance about the work you have set before me. Set my heart on your promise to be with me and to bless the work I do in your name. Amen.

M.J.S.

For further reading, see The People's Bible commentary on Exodus, pages 20-30.

When Faithfulness Makes It Harder

Bible Reading: Exodus 4:18–5:21

Pharaoh said, "Who is the LORD, that I should obey him and let Israel go? I do not know the LORD and I will not let Israel go." (Exodus 5:2)

When Moses poured out objections at the burning bush, the Lord promised to go with him. Through Moses, the Lord would deliver his people and keep his covenant with Abraham, Isaac, and Jacob.

But when Moses stood before Pharaoh and spoke in the name of the Lord, everything seemed to go sideways. The king shrugged off the demand. He was the god of Egypt. He did not know the Lord and would not submit to him.

But for Moses, this was worse than mere rejection. Pharaoh retaliated. He increased the Israelites' workload and their misery. Moses was caught in the middle between an irate Pharaoh and exasperated Israelites. The people he had been sent to rescue called down curses on him.

If the Lord really is sovereign and faithful and unchanging, then what was going on here? Maybe you've wondered the same. You carry out the work he's given you to do, but it seems only to make things worse—especially for you!

Jesus' words to his 72 missionaries are helpful here: "Whoever listens to you listens to me; whoever rejects you rejects me; but whoever rejects me rejects him who sent me" (Luke 10:16). Pharaoh wasn't just rejecting Moses; he was rejecting the Lord who sent him. Moses wasn't in this position because God had left him but because God had sent him.

The Lord does not send his people on fools' errands—even if everything seems in vain. He always accomplishes his good purpose. Pharaoh objected, "I do not know the LORD." But on account of his hard heart, he was about to learn. Through the deliverance of Israel and the judgment of Egypt, God would display his power and his name would be proclaimed in all the earth.

When your faithfulness seems to be in vain, remember who has sent you. Jesus accomplished God's purpose and your salvation through his rejection and crucifixion. He was vindicated through his resurrection. His was no fool's errand. And neither is the work God has set before you, no matter how it seems in the moment.

Prayer: Dear Jesus, give me joy and confidence in the work you have set before me. Even when it results in thanklessness and rejection, you will accomplish your good purposes through it. Amen.

M.J.S.

For further reading, see The People's Bible commentary on Exodus, pages 30-36.

Faith Waits on the Lord

Bible Reading: Exodus 5:22–7:7

God also said to Moses, "I am the LORD." (Exodus 6:2)

Pharaoh refused to heed the Lord's command: "Who is the LORD, that I should obey him and let Israel go? I do not know the LORD and I will not let Israel go" (Exodus 5:2).

But Pharaoh wasn't the only one who underestimated the Lord. At the first sign of setback, Moses complained that the mission was a failure. He didn't see any deliverance—only more trouble.

God responded to Moses' accusations by setting a simple sentence on Moses' heart and on his lips: "I am the LORD." Note the capital letters. That's how most English translations of the Bible identify God's special name for himself. The name stresses his faithfulness to his promises. Simply put, "the LORD" means Savior.

Count how many times God said "I am the LORD" in these verses. He said it to Moses and assured him that he was about to see God's faithfulness to the promises made to Abraham, Isaac, and Jacob. Moses' ancestors had held on to those promises by faith. Moses was about to see them fulfilled.

He told Moses to say it to the Israelites: "I am the LORD" (Exodus 6:6). They were about to see God's outstretched arm and mighty acts of judgment on behalf of his chosen people. Their faith (together with their doubts) would soon give way to sight.

Egypt was about to see it too. The god of Egypt would soon experience the devastation of standing against the God who was relentless in keeping his promises. "The Egyptians will know that I am the LORD when I stretch out my hand against Egypt and bring the Israelites out of it" (Exodus 7:5).

Again, "the LORD" means Savior. "I am the LORD" is a call to faith. It redirects our hearts to the only One who can rescue us. God is reminding his people, "No matter how things look right now, I haven't forgotten. Nothing can stand in my way. I am going to save you."

Such faith waits on the Lord. It's not a matter of *if.* It's only a matter of *when.* He will prove himself faithful. And when our wait is over, it will forever be clear that our salvation was his work, not ours.

Prayer: Heavenly Father, when my heart grows weary and my faith is overwhelmed with doubt, redirect me to you, my only Savior. My help comes from the Lord, the Maker of heaven and earth. Amen.

M.J.S.

For further reading, see The People's Bible commentary on Exodus, pages 33-46.

The Delusion of a Hard Heart

Bible Reading: Exodus 7:8–8:32

When Pharaoh saw that there was relief, he hardened his heart and would not listen to Moses and Aaron, just as the LORD had said. (Exodus 8:15)

The Lord acted just as he said he would. He stretched out his hand and unleashed mighty acts of judgment against Egypt. Pharaoh was helpless against the acts of God. Granted, his magicians could mimic the first two plagues with their dark arts. But what did that accomplish? These magicians could only add to the disaster. They could not provide relief.

There was no denying the Lord's hand in the plagues. He announced them in advance. He provided relief at his word—he would spare his own people while the nation around them was ravaged. Soon enough, Pharaoh's own advisors warned him, "This is the finger of God" (8:19). They could see that the god of Egypt was no match for the God of Israel.

So why couldn't Pharaoh see it? He was driving his nation into the ground, convinced that he was going to come out on top! That's the nature of a hard heart. Pharaoh's problem wasn't subpar intelligence. It was a corrupted will that would not bend to reality—no matter how clear God made it. Pharaoh set himself in the place of God, and he would not yield the position. He hardened his heart.

This is a sobering example of what we confess about ourselves in worship: "I am sinful by nature." Sin isn't a blemish on the surface of the heart. It's deep, unbending opposition to God that will not listen to reason.

Through Pharaoh's heart God provides a much-needed warning for us. Our sin is not to be taken lightly. God's will is not to be shrugged off. We aren't in control of sin. Sin controls us. If we think otherwise, we're delusional.

Because our sin is a part of us, our deliverance must come from outside of us. This deliverance comes from the Lord. The very same God whom our hearts, by nature, hate "so loved the world that he gave his one and only Son, that whoever believes in him shall not perish but have eternal life" (John 3:16).

Prayer: Dear Savior, today I confess in particular my flagrant sins. I've dismissed your warnings. I've engaged in evil on purpose. Forgive me for Jesus' sake. Create in me a clean heart and renew me in the image of my Creator. Amen.

M.J.S.

For further reading, see The People's Bible commentary on Exodus, pages 44-54.

The Lord Is the Hero of Our Story

Bible Reading: Exodus chapters 9 and 10

Then the Lord said to Moses, "Go to Pharaoh, for I have hardened his heart and the hearts of his officials so that I may perform these signs of mine among them [2] that you may tell your children and grandchildren how I dealt harshly with the Egyptians and how I performed my signs among them, and that you may know that I am the Lord." (Exodus 10:1-2)

Pharaoh's hard heart is a major theme in the Exodus account. It's mentioned more than ten times. But there's a shift as the story progresses. During the earlier plagues, it says that Pharaoh hardened his heart. During the latter plagues, it says that the Lord hardened Pharaoh's heart. The Lord handed Pharaoh over to his sin. Since Pharaoh was determined to march down this road to his own destruction, God finally removed every off-ramp.

God's hardening of Pharaoh's heart was an act of judgment. But it also served to glorify the Lord and to testify to his faithfulness through the generations. No one could ever give Pharaoh credit for Israel's liberation. The Israelites didn't go free by the goodness of his heart. His heart spurned God's deliverance, and the god of Egypt could not prevent the Lord from keeping his covenant with Abraham, with Isaac, and with Jacob.

There's only one hero in this story. When God called Moses, Moses tried to get out of it. When God confronted Pharaoh, he hardened Pharoah's heart. As soon as the Israelites got out of Egypt, they started complaining about their present circumstances and singing the praises of Egypt. The only reason the Israelites were the people of God was that God had made them his people. He's the hero. It's his work from beginning to end.

That's the only way it could ever be. The glory always belongs to God. Not with Israel. Not with us. He gives, and no one can stop him. We receive, not because of our worthiness but because he is the Lord. He is faithful to his promises.

Tell your children and your grandchildren what the Lord has done for you. And for them.

Prayer: Lord God, keep pride far from my heart. Let my heart find rest in you alone, the only God and Savior. Let my whole life be a testimony to your glory. Amen.

M.J.S.

For further reading, see The People's Bible commentary on Exodus, pages 54-63.

Saved by the Blood of the Lamb

Bible Reading: Exodus 11:1–12:30

"On that same night I will pass through Egypt and strike down every firstborn of both people and animals, and I will bring judgment on all the gods of Egypt. I am the LORD. [13] The blood will be a sign for you on the houses where you are, and when I see the blood, I will pass over you. No destructive plague will touch you when I strike Egypt." (Exodus 12:12-13)

God's judgment and his deliverance go hand in hand. To rescue the good guys, God took out the bad guys. He crushed Egypt, and Israel went free.

But what made God consider the Israelites good? So far in Exodus little has been disclosed about their moral character. The emphasis has been on their weakness and misery. There's nothing virtuous about victimhood. As the rest of the Exodus account unfolds, we're given more insight into their character. It's generally not pretty.

God didn't rescue the Israelites because of their character. He rescued them because he had chosen them. He's the Lord, and he had made a promise to Abraham, Isaac, and Jacob—a promise that went all the way back to Adam and Eve in the garden. Through their offspring, he would crush the serpent's head and all nations on earth would be blessed. Delivering Israel from Egypt was part of God's plan to bring the Savior of all.

Israel's preparation for the final plague testified to it. When the Lord passed through Egypt to deliver death to every house, he passed over the houses with the blood of the lamb on their door frames. Not because the people inside were more virtuous but because a lamb had been sacrificed for that house. That's why God considered them good. Their sin was paid for. Forgiven.

The annual commemoration would remind the Israelites why God had rescued them and provide them opportunities to teach their children. It would also teach them about the deliverance to come—the Lamb of God who would take away the sin of the world. On the cross, God would sacrifice this Lamb. And all who believe in him would go free.

Prayer: Dear Jesus, thank you for giving your life for mine. I belong to you not because of my virtue but because of your redemption. Grant that I always find my peace in you alone and lead a life that reflects your faithful love. Amen.

M.J.S.

For further reading, see The People's Bible commentary on Exodus, pages 63-74.

The Lord Is Always on His Throne

Bible Reading: Exodus 12:31-50

During the night Pharaoh summoned Moses and Aaron and said, "Up! Leave my people, you and the Israelites! Go, worship the LORD as you have requested." (Exodus 12:31)

[35] **The Israelites did as Moses instructed and asked the Egyptians for articles of silver and gold and for clothing.** [36] **The LORD had made the Egyptians favorably disposed toward the people, and they gave them what they asked for; so they plundered the Egyptians.** (Exodus 12:35-36)

Psalm 2 describes the most powerful people on earth joining forces against the Lord. God's response? He laughs. He dashes them to pieces like a clay pot on concrete.

It doesn't always seem as though the Lord and his chosen ones will prevail. When the pharaoh to whom Joseph meant nothing deemed the Israelites a national security threat, the king oppressed them with forced labor. He murdered their children. They groaned under slavery for hundreds of years. When the Lord said through Moses, "Let my people go," Pharaoh scoffed, "Who is the LORD?" and made their work even worse (Exodus 5:1-2). For so long it seemed as if the god of Egypt was mightier than the God of Israel.

But the Lord laughed from his throne in heaven. Pharaoh's measures to contain Israel brought about the devastation of his nation and the death of his own son. When God's people walked away from the ruins that were once the most powerful nation on earth, the Egyptians lavished them with precious gifts—effectively back pay for their labor.

It sounds incredible, but none of it should have been a surprise. This wasn't God making a comeback in the fourth quarter. This was the Lord fulfilling the promise he had given to Abraham five hundred years earlier (Genesis 15:13-16) and to Moses at the burning bush (Exodus 3:18-22).

When we consider the state of our world, our nation, our families, or our churches, it may seem to us as though God isn't in control, as though evil is going to prevail. But the Lord is on his throne in heaven—always, even when we're weak and hurting and wondering. He has given us his promise. He has given us his Son. You can trust him. And when Jesus returns in glory, you'll see.

Prayer: Lord Jesus, keep me from using my circumstances to measure your love and faithfulness. Open my eyes to see your love in your death for me and in your rule over all things for me. Be my strength in my weakness. When the time is right, do away with evil forever and usher in the age to come. Amen.

M.J.S.

For further reading, see The People's Bible commentary on Exodus, pages 72-75.

The "Whys" Behind the Rituals

Bible Reading: Exodus 13:1-16

"In days to come, when your son asks you, 'What does this mean?' say to him, 'With a mighty hand the LORD brought us out of Egypt, out of the land of slavery. 15 When Pharaoh stubbornly refused to let us go, the LORD killed the firstborn of both people and animals in Egypt. This is why I sacrifice to the LORD the first male offspring of every womb and redeem each of my firstborn sons.' 16 And it will be like a sign on your hand and a symbol on your forehead that the LORD brought us out of Egypt with his mighty hand." (Exodus 13:14-16)

Every year when spring bloomed in the Promised Land, God's redeemed people would sweep the yeast out of their homes, slaughter an unblemished lamb, and celebrate the Passover. It was like their Fourth of July. They celebrated in order to remember where they came from and to teach their children who they were. They did it because of what the Lord did for them when they came out of Egypt (13:8).

God provided another opportunity to remember his deliverance: Every firstborn male among the Israelites was to be set apart for him. In the case of most livestock, the firstborn male was to be sacrificed. It belonged to the Lord. In the case of humans, the firstborn son was to be redeemed. He too belonged to the Lord. The parents would buy him back, so to speak, at a price of five shekels of silver (Numbers 18:16).

It seems so strange! The children who observed the ritual would certainly ask questions: "Why are we doing this?" And the parents could answer by teaching them how the Lord brought them out of Egypt: "He killed every firstborn of Egyptian people and animals, but he spared our homes. That means we belong to him."

A similar scene might play out today. A young child watches her parents give an offering at church. It seems so strange: "Why are we doing this?" And the parents respond by teaching her about their God who redeemed them from sin with his holy, precious blood and with his innocent suffering and death: "All this he did that we should be his own. Our offering is a token that all we are and have belongs to him."

Prayer: Heavenly Father, surround me with opportunities to demonstrate with my life that you have redeemed me and that I am a child of the only gracious God. Amen.

M.J.S.

For further reading, see The People's Bible commentary on Exodus, pages 75-78.

Even When Faith Falters, God's Glory Shines

Bible Reading: Exodus 13:17–14:31

Moses answered the people, "Do not be afraid. Stand firm and you will see the deliverance the LORD will bring you today. The Egyptians you see today you will never see again. 14 The LORD will fight for you; you need only to be still." (Exodus 14:13-14)

The Lord had done it! After 430 years in Egypt, the Israelites were on their way to the Promised Land. They could *see* God at the helm, his presence manifested in a pillar of cloud by day and a pillar of fire by night. He had done it. They were free at last!

But God intended to glorify himself through Egypt one more time in a most spectacular way. He lured Egypt in. He led his people into a vulnerable position and hardened Pharaoh's heart so that he took chase. It looked like a tactical nightmare for the Israelites. They were sandwiched between the Red Sea on one side and the best of Pharaoh's army closing in on them from the other.

The Israelites berated Moses. Despite the ten plagues, it was as if they had never seen the Lord in action. Despite the pillar of cloud, it was as if the Lord wasn't even there. They were already singing about the good old days in Egypt.

But their despondence would not stand in the way of the Lord letting his glory shine. He did it all. They just watched and walked a red carpet out of the land of slavery. The same water that stood aside for them crushed their foes. The glory belonged to the Lord.

We may wonder why God would orchestrate such a desperate situation in the first place. He was establishing a track record. It's evidence that we can trust him. One of God's favorite phrases in the Bible is "do not be afraid." He doesn't say it because there is no danger or because things aren't as bad as we imagine. He says it because he's faithful and powerful and on our side: "Don't be afraid. I'm with you. I will not fail you."

The greater the trouble, the greater the opportunity for God to display his glory. It's not by our strength. It's by his. He is the Lord.

Prayer: Lord God, when I meditate on your great acts of power and faithfulness and forgiveness in the Bible, open my eyes of faith to realize that you are just as powerful and faithful and forgiving for me. Amen.

M.J.S.

For further reading, see The People's Bible commentary on Exodus, pages 78-87.

Israel's Grumbling Begins

Bible Reading: Exodus chapter 15

Then Moses led Israel from the Red Sea and they
went into the Desert of Shur. For three days they
traveled in the desert without finding water. 23 When
they came to Marah, they could not drink its water
because it was bitter. (That is why the place is called
Marah.) 24 So the people grumbled against Moses,
saying, "What are we to drink?" (Exodus 15:22-24)

Heartfelt praise abounds in most of chapter 15. On the far side of the Red Sea, the Israelites praised the Lord with song and dance. His glory was their salvation. The trust in their hearts poured forth from their lips.

But they got thirsty. After three days without an oasis, their reserves were empty and their lips were parched. When they finally found a spring, the water wasn't potable. In the desert, they learned quickly that water is life. Without it there would soon be more than a million corpses littering the ground at Marah.

It was then that they changed their tune. In their desperation, the sin in their hearts poured forth from their lips. The grumbling began.

Their grumbling didn't stop the Lord from providing. But that didn't mean it was no big deal. Grumbling is the coward's rebellion. So the Lord warned them that they ought not let his deliverance go to their heads. If they hardened their hearts as Pharaoh did, they would suffer the same fate.

God's Spirit renews the Christian's heart in the image of its Creator. But how quickly the heart reverts to its old ways. Our sinful natures are eager to pervert God's grace into license, to convince us that our suffering gives us a right to lash out at God and at others. God's warnings aren't empty threats. Just keep reading Israel's history and compare it to 1 Corinthians 10:1-13.

God warns us because he loves us. He knows what we're capable of. The ultimate purpose of his warnings is to bring us ever closer to himself in repentant faith. "I am the LORD, who heals you" (Exodus 15:26).

Prayer: Dear Lord, for every commandment I have flouted and for every sin I have taken lightly, I have no one to blame but myself. I repent. Forgive me for Jesus' sake. Defend me from every evil, keep me close to you, and bring me through every trial to my eternal home with you. Amen.

M.J.S.

For further reading, see The People's Bible commentary on Exodus, pages 88-94.

Give Us Today Our Daily Bread

Bible Reading: Exodus chapter 16

The Israelites ate manna forty years, until they came to a land that was settled; they ate manna until they reached the border of Canaan. (Exodus 16:35)

In spite of God's warning at Marah, Israel's grumbling only grew worse. The Israelites preferred Pharaoh's tyranny over the Lord's deliverance.

Instead of responding with a plague, the Lord showed them how different he and Pharaoh were. When Pharaoh sensed discontent, he oppressed the Israelites even more by taking away their straw. When the Israelites griped at the Lord, he provided—not to indulge their grumbling but to demonstrate his grace in spite of it.

The Lord showered them with bread from heaven for the next 40 years. Notice how he did it: one day at a time. Every day they received enough for that day. He was not just filling their bellies. He was teaching them trust. When they went to bed, their cupboards were empty. But when they got up, there was more bread on the ground.

Friday was an exception: They were to gather twice as much and keep the leftovers overnight to eat on the Sabbath. The Lord wasn't a taskmaster like Pharaoh who cared only about their output. He provided for them in abundance and cared about their rest—in spite of their calloused complaining. Their yearning for Egypt was baseless.

Forty years later at the edge of the Promised Land, Moses would recall God's purpose in all this. It was to teach them "that man does not live on bread alone but on every word that comes from the mouth of the Lord" (Deuteronomy 8:3). For 40 years they went to bed with empty cupboards. They didn't have any bread, but they could rest in peace because they had a promise from the mouth of God. Bread would cover the ground again the next day. They could trust him.

We tend to look for security in stored-up goods: a paid-off house and a financial portfolio that will outlive us. But that's turning gifts into gods. There's something better. We have a Father God who invites us to pray: "Give us today our daily bread." It's not just a prayer. It's a promise. For however many days he gives us on this earth, he'll keep it.

Prayer: Almighty Father, provide what I need for each day. Fill me with trust that you will provide it. Amen.

M.J.S.

For further reading, see The People's Bible commentary on Exodus, pages 94-100.

The Gracious Lord Warns the Hard-Hearted

Bible Reading: Exodus 17:1-7

[The Israelites] camped at Rephidim, but there was no water for the people to drink. 2 So they quarreled with Moses and said, "Give us water to drink."

Moses replied, "Why do you quarrel with me? Why do you put the LORD to the test?" (Exodus 17:1-2)

The continual whining made for a tired refrain. Moses couldn't seem to catch a break. Pharaoh was out of the picture, but now Israel played the role of Moses' enemy. Moses realized that the people's quarrel was really with God: "Why do you put the LORD to the test?" But he was still caught in the middle. He sensed that they were on the verge of murdering him.

God's miraculous provision of water satisfied the Israelites' need, but there was also a warning implicit in it. When God instructed Moses to strike the rock with his staff, the Lord identified it as the same staff with which Moses had struck the Nile. The Lord provided water in a waterless place by using the same power with which he had removed it from the earth's most fertile river. Once again, his grace abounded.

But do not receive his grace in vain. This warning at the rock echoes for all God's people in Psalm 95:7-9: "Today, if only you would hear his voice, 'Do not harden your hearts as you did at Meribah, as you did that day at Massah in the wilderness, where your ancestors tested me; they tried me, though they had seen what I did.'" Pharaoh wasn't the only sinner capable of hardening his heart. Our nature is the same. We also must beware. Everyone who sins is a slave to sin.

Listen to the Lord's warnings. He's speaking them to you for the purpose of calling you to himself. He's your only way out. He will not fail you: "If the Son sets you free, you will be free indeed" (John 8:36).

Prayer: Holy Spirit, guard me from underestimating my inclination to evil and the power of sin to harden my heart. Through Jesus' death for me, give me the peace of his forgiveness and fill me with strength to lead a life that brings glory to you. Amen.

M.J.S.

For further reading, see The People's Bible commentary on Exodus, pages 100-103.

God's Grace Is for the Undeserving

Bible Reading: Exodus 17:8-16

So Joshua fought the Amalekites as Moses had ordered, and Moses, Aaron and Hur went to the top of the hill. [11]As long as Moses held up his hands, the Israelites were winning, but whenever he lowered his hands, the Amalekites were winning. (Exodus 17:10-11)

The Lord delivered the Israelites from slavery. He was escorting them to a land flowing with milk and honey. But, apart from their singing and dancing on the far side of the Red Sea, their only recorded response was complaining.

It's enough to turn the reader of Exodus against them: *How could they be so untrusting, so thankless, so blasphemous? If I were God, I would have given up on them long ago. They don't deserve this!*

And that's the point. The Israelites' liberation from slavery, their survival in the desert, their designation as the Lord's own people—none of it was due to their virtue or strength or worthiness. It was the Lord's faithful love from beginning to end.

When an enemy army tried to exploit God's vulnerable people, his faithful love shone again. Without question, the Amalekites were a superior force. Just watch what happened when Moses grew too weary to uphold the staff of God. No one could deny that the victory was the Lord's.

What was more incredible: the lengths to which God was willing to go to keep his promise or the kind of people to whom God was willing to keep his promise? His zeal for the weak and complaining Israelites was beyond comprehension. He would not tolerate another nation trying to exploit his chosen people. He vowed to blot out the Amalekites from under heaven.

We've certainly given the people who know us best reason to wonder, *How could they be so untrusting, so thankless, so blasphemous?* Surely we've all thought it ourselves: *If I were God, I would have given up on me long ago.*

But just like Israel, we're not the heroes of our own story. Instead of giving us what we deserve or blessing us according to our strength, God gives and blesses according to his promises in Christ Jesus. It's the Lord's faithful love from beginning to end. God's grace isn't about what we deserve. That's what makes it grace.

Prayer: Lord Jesus, keep both self-righteousness and doubt far from my heart. You are my strength, my forgiveness, my confidence, and my life. Amen.

M.J.S.

For further reading, see The People's Bible commentary on Exodus, pages 103-105.

The Benefits of Sharing the Burden

Bible Reading: Exodus chapter 18

Moses' father-in-law replied, "What you are doing is not good. [18]You and these people who come to you will only wear yourselves out. The work is too heavy for you; you cannot handle it alone." (Exodus 18:17-18)

Before God finished his work on the sixth day of creation, he observed Adam and said, "It is not good for the man to be alone. I will make a helper suitable for him" (Genesis 2:18). When Jethro observed Moses trying to serve as the sole judge of Israel, he used the same Hebrew phrase: "What you are doing is not good." The similarity extends beyond the choice of words. God didn't create people to be islands. He designed us to complement one another and to work together.

Moses was taking on too much. It was a disservice both to him and to the people he served. He was worn out from working. The people were worn out by waiting. Israel's judicial system was backlogged.

Jethro offered sound counsel. Moses could delegate the work without shirking his responsibilities. Israel had capable men who were God-fearing and trustworthy. Moses could appoint them to be suitable helpers. They could take the easier cases; the most difficult could land on his desk. The burden was distributed. The people were better served.

Are you in a position of leadership? God hasn't left you to do it all by yourself. Are there capable people around you who have the maturity and gifts to help you? Maybe you should ask them.

Has God placed you under someone else's leadership? He hasn't left your leaders to do it all by themselves. How could you use the gifts God has given you to help leaders shoulder their burdens? Maybe you should ask them.

The Christian church is like a body. Jesus is the head. We're the various parts with various functions, all of us loved by Jesus and called to serve one another with love. When we work together, it's *good.*

Prayer: Holy Spirit, through Baptism you have made me part of the body of Christ. You have given me gifts to serve and have surrounded me with people to serve. Give me a selfless heart, use me to bring your blessing to the body, use the body to bring blessing to me, and use all of it to your glory. Amen.

M.J.S.

For further reading, see The People's Bible commentary on Exodus, pages 105-110.

A Holy People for a Holy God

Bible Reading: Exodus chapter 19

"Now if you obey me fully and keep my covenant, then out of all nations you will be my treasured possession. Although the whole earth is mine, [6]you will be for me a kingdom of priests and a holy nation." (Exodus 19:5-6)

The Israelites arrived at Mt. Sinai. Forty years earlier, the Lord had appeared to Moses at this same place in the burning bush. God had told him to take off his sandals and keep his distance. The presence of the Lord made this holy ground.

That God is holy means that he is in a league of his own. He is superlative majesty—even angels cover their faces in his presence. He is superlative morality—he loves good and hates evil.

The Israelites were about to get a taste of God's holiness, much as Moses had. As God had made Moses take off his sandals, the people were to make special preparations for the event. Above all, they shouldn't get too close and perish! There was no such thing as a casual encounter with God.

But just as with Moses, God had a holy purpose for the Israelites. He carried them out of slavery in Egypt to make a covenant with them. God's obligation: Out of all the nations, they would be his treasured possession, a holy nation, in a league of their own. Their obligation: They must obey him fully. They must be holy, as the Lord their God is holy. Their lives were to be a reflection of him for all the world to see.

We don't have to read much further to see it all fall apart—over and over again. The covenant wasn't the problem. The Israelites were. They broke his covenant.

Sinners cannot have a relationship with a holy God if it depends on their obedience. Holiness cannot be drawn from a sinful heart. We need a different kind of covenant—one that depends on God alone. We need God to give us more than rules. We need him to give us holiness itself.

Prayer: Father in heaven, Jesus is the only reason I can approach a holy God as my Father. I have broken your law, but he obeyed in my place. I deserve your punishment, but he died in my place. Continue to transform my heart through his forgiveness so that all my life may be a reflection of you. Amen.

M.J.S.

For further reading, see The People's Bible commentary on Exodus, pages 111-119.

The Lord Is a Jealous God

Bible Reading: Exodus chapter 20

"I, the LORD your God, am a jealous God, punishing the children for the sin of the parents to the third and fourth generation of those who hate me,
6 but showing love to a thousand generations of those who love me and keep my commandments." (Exodus 20:5-6)

Verses 5-6 serve as an exclamation point for the First Commandment—really, for all the commandments. God takes disobedience and obedience seriously. This wasn't the whimpering of a vacillating guru. Israel was entering into a covenant with a jealous God.

Jealousy carries a negative connotation for us—it's to wrongfully desire something that doesn't belong to us. But it's different with God. That God is jealous means he wants what *does* belong to him. He brought the Israelites out of the land of slavery. He was their God. They were his people. If they gave their hearts to anything else, he would punish them. If they loved and trusted him and showed it in their obedience to his commandments, his love would abide.

There's a special warning here for parents. If they give their hearts to other gods and disregard God's commandments, their children will learn to do the same. The parents' sins will continue to haunt their family for generations to come.

God gives us his law because he's jealous for us. He will not tolerate anything that comes between him and his people, and that's what sin does. So God promises to punish all who break his commandments and to teach others to do the same. If that seems overly harsh to us, then we do not comprehend the evil of sin and the love of God. No one can accuse the Lord of ambivalence.

Apart from the cross of Christ, the Ten Commandments only condemn us. God's exclamation point removes any hope that he will let sin slide.

But the cross changed everything. Our jealous God punished his own Son for our sin. Jesus took it all in our place. At the same time, Jesus credited his love for God and his obedience to us. Because of Jesus, all God has for us is love. No ambivalence. Only jealous, enduring love that will not let anything come between him and his people.

Prayer: Lord God, deliver me from every temptation to dismiss your holy law. Use my words and actions to teach the next generation that you mean what you say. By your Spirit, teach me to find certainty of your love in Christ alone and to honor you with obedience that demonstrates your love at work in my heart. Amen.

M.J.S.

For further reading, see The People's Bible commentary on Exodus, pages 119-127.

The Book of the Covenant

Bible Reading: Exodus chapters 21–23

"These are the laws you are to set before them." (Exodus 21:1)

The Ten Commandments were a primary component of the Lord's covenant with Israel. God spoke them with his own voice from the mountain. He engraved them on tablets of stone with his own finger.

But there was more to this covenant than the Ten Commandments. Over the next three chapters, God spells out laws that Moses was to present to the people. These were written on a scroll that came to be called the Book of the Covenant (Exodus 24:7). Many of the laws sound strange to our ears. Some, such as regulations for slavery, are downright offensive from our American perspective.

To gain a proper understanding, it helps to look for common themes. In general, the laws were applications of the Ten Commandments to specific cases: "If such-and-such happens, then you must address it by doing such-and-such." But more important than recognizing the written structure of the laws is to recognize their purpose: Their purpose was to protect people. These laws protected the rights of the disadvantaged from being abused by the powerful. They protected the nation from wickedness that could infect and kill it. They even protected wrongdoers from suffering punishments that could exceed what was appropriate for their crimes. Most crucially, the laws prescribed worship regulations to protect the Israelites from forgetting and forsaking their God.

The Israelites didn't just need protection against threats from the outside—hunger, thirst, natural catastrophes, enemy nations. They needed protection against themselves. Even God's redeemed people had hearts bent on sin, and it is the nature of sin to destroy. These laws were designed to curb their sinful desires and to keep their eyes of faith focused on their God who forgives and renews the hearts of the forgiven into his image.

Blessed is the nation whose laws protect its people by restraining their sinful actions.

Prayer: Heavenly Father, bless my nation with legislators who enact laws that curb sin. Bless my nation with executives who carry out these laws for the good of its residents. Bless my nation with judges who promote justice. Bless me with a heart that respects them all and that seeks to live a quiet life in all godliness and holiness. Amen.

M.J.S.

For further reading, see The People's Bible commentary on Exodus, pages 127-144.

The Blood of the Covenant

Bible Reading: Exodus chapter 24

[The Israelite men] offered burnt offerings and
sacrificed young bulls as fellowship offerings to the
Lord. 6 Moses took half of the blood and put it in
bowls, and the other half he splashed against the altar.
7 Then he took the Book of the Covenant and read it
to the people. They responded, "We will do everything the Lord has said; we will obey."

8 Moses then took the blood, sprinkled it on the
people and said, "This is the blood of the covenant that the Lord has made with you in accordance with all these words." (Exodus 24:5-8)

When the Israelites first arrived at Mount Sinai, God introduced his covenant with them: "If you obey me fully and keep my covenant, then out of all nations you will be my treasured possession" (Exodus 19:5). If they kept their end, God would keep his. Now that God had laid out the terms, it was time for the people to sign on the dotted line.

The people gathered at the base of the mountain and expressed their assent with one voice: "We will do everything the LORD has said; we will obey."

Then came the blood. They had collected it from the sacrifices of countless animals. Half of it they splashed against the altar, the other half on the people. This "blood of the covenant" purified the Israelites to be God's holy people so that they could carry out their holy calling. It also bound them to their obligations and God to his. They were swearing on their lives. This was serious business.

But these were not the only animals ever slain in Israel's worship. Israel's need for purification was ongoing because their obedience always fell short—far short! And so blood was always flowing. Always more blood!

When Jesus instituted his Supper on the night before he died on the cross, he borrowed language from Exodus chapter 24: "Drink from it, all of you. This is *MY blood of the covenant,* which is poured out for many for the forgiveness of sins" (Matthew 26:27-28; emphasis added). It wasn't the blood of livestock offered again and again. This was God's own blood, poured out a single time for a single purpose: "for the forgiveness of sins."

What you receive in the Lord's Supper isn't a symbol of your obedience to God. It's not an if-you-keep-your-end-God-will-keep-his-end kind of covenant. God is the doer. You are the receiver. Your sins are forgiven because Jesus died for you.

Prayer: Dear Jesus, with your own holy blood you have reconciled me to God. Let my confidence always rest on your works and not on my own. Let my life reflect your holy will. Amen.

M.J.S.

For further reading, see The People's Bible commentary on Exodus, pages 144-149.

Sacred Things

Bible Reading: Exodus chapters 25-27

"Then have [the Israelites] make a sanctuary for me, and I will dwell among them. [9] Make this tabernacle and all its furnishings exactly like the pattern I will show you." (Exodus 25:8-9)

God's covenant with the people of Israel was like a marriage. They promised to love and be faithful to each other. And now, like a happy couple at the beginning of their married life together, it was time to start living together. So God gave Moses instructions for how to make a home for God.

That's what we read about in Exodus chapters 25–27. God gave Moses instructions for a tabernacle: a tent that would serve as a house of worship during their wanderings in the wilderness. Think of it as a starter home until it was time for something more permanent.

And God told Moses how to furnish the home too. God gave the Israelites instructions for how to build holy things, furnishings of fine wood and precious metals, each with a purpose to serve. There was an ark, or chest, where their most precious documents and keepsakes would be stored and where God would speak to his people; a table for loaves of bread representing the tribes, because families gather together at a table; a lamp representing the Spirit so his house would be filled with light; an altar so that the home would be a place of forgiveness.

In a sense, these holy things were all just things. But they were designed to serve sacred purposes as God and his people lived together. This was God's furniture, making his house a home to share with his people. And when God uses something for his purposes, he makes it holy.

You'll see the same in your church: a table to gather around for God's meal, candles to remind us of God's light and his Spirit, a cross that calls to mind Christ's sacrifice. Find the same in your house too: a dinner table where the Bible is read after meals, the bedside where prayers are spoken as a family. They're just things, fashioned of wood and metal, but they serve holy purposes. They show us that even though we've fallen and broken our covenant with God, he still makes his home among us.

Prayer: Heavenly Father, you fill heaven and earth and have no need of houses built by human hands. Yet your greatest joy is to be with your people. Take the things of our churches and our homes and make them holy—put your furniture to sacred use as you live with us. Amen.

J.C.S.

For further reading, see The People's Bible commentary on Exodus, pages 150-176.

You're on Christ's Heart

Bible Reading: Exodus chapter 28

"Whenever Aaron enters the Holy Place, he will bear the names of the sons of Israel over his heart on the breastpiece of decision as a continuing memorial before the Lord." (Exodus 28:29)

Judges wear robes. Officers wear uniforms. Doctors wear scrubs. What they wear sets them apart from the rest of the people. Is their clothing ceremonial or functional? It's often a bit of both.

So it was with the high priest. The high priest—Moses' brother Aaron would be the first—was the one man to represent the nation of Israel before God on the most holy festivals and to represent God to the nation of Israel. The high priest was a go-between, a mediator between God and humans.

And God had him dress the part. Everything about the priest's clothes served a purpose. Some of the beauty was just to give him dignity and honor, but some elements of his clothing were used as he sought after God's will. He was dressed in white linen, in blue and purple, with ropes of braided gold.

But your eyes would have been drawn to his chest. The high priest was to wear a special breastpiece. On it were four rows of precious stones with three stones in each row; each stone was engraved with the name of one of the twelve tribes of Israel.

Some of the symbolism in Israel's worship life was subtle, but not this. As the high priest ministered before the Lord, he brought the Israelites with him into God's presence. He was their representative to God. And when he spoke for God, there was to be no doubt about what mattered to God. God carried his people on his heart. And like emeralds or topaz or onyx, they were precious to him—his own treasure.

We all carry so much on our hearts. We have our fears, our failures, and the needs of our families and our friends. We carry guilt from sins past and anxieties about the days to come. The New Testament book of Hebrews tells us that the high priest was just a symbol of our Savior. Jesus, the great mediator, goes to the Father in heaven on our behalf. He stands before God as he ministers for us, and the robes of the high priest tell us why he's there. Jesus takes you with him, together with all your sins and all your worries. He carries you with him to God. You're on his heart. You are precious to him.

Prayer: Lord Jesus, whatever weighs on me today—my sins, my fears, my needs—take it on your heart, take it to the Father, and bring the Father's love to me. Amen.

J.C.S.

For further reading, see The People's Bible commentary on Exodus, pages 176-183.

God's Grace to Begin and End the Day

Bible Reading: Exodus chapter 29

"This is what you are to offer on the altar regularly each day: two lambs a year old. 39 Offer one in the morning and the other at twilight." (Exodus 29:38-39)

Martin Luther wrote a set of morning and evening prayers. His prayers lead us to thank God for the protection he gives to our bodies and our souls alike as he guards us from danger, keeps us from evil, and forgives our sins. Luther encouraged believers, as they began and ended their days with those prayers, to mark themselves with the sign of the cross as they prayed: "In the name of the Father and of the Son and of the Holy Spirit."

Those words and that action are reminders of our baptisms. When we wake up in the morning facing a day filled with possibilities, we remember who we are: dearly loved children of God, washed clean in Baptism, set apart for lives of serving God. When we prepare for bed with another day behind us, we remember what God has done: He's not only spared us from punishment throughout the day, but he's forgiven the evil we've done and the good we've failed to do. We stand clean in our baptismal grace, and we're prepared to lie down and sleep in peace.

Luther's pattern of morning and evening prayers wasn't new. As the Lord gave instructions for how the priests were to be set apart for service to him, he also gave directions for one of their most important functions. Every morning and evening the priest was to offer a sacrifice for the sins of Israel. The type of sacrifice God directed the priest to offer proclaimed several important messages at once: God accepted a sacrifice of a lamb in the Israelites' place; their sins were forgiven; God was in joyful communion with Israel; the people of Israel were giving thanks to God for his goodness. Every day began and ended with those precious truths.

It's good that occasions in our life prompt us to pray to God. We ask his blessings at births and weddings and graduations; we seek his help in hospital rooms and at gravesites; we pray for his grace when we fall into sin. But our relationship with God is a daily matter. Because of the sacrifice of Jesus, the Lamb of God, we can live every day devoted to his service, and his love and forgiveness for us is never failing. That's the gift God gives: every day begun and ended in his grace.

Prayer: Father, Son, and Holy Spirit, help me live today to your glory, and at its close, let me fall asleep in your peace. Through Jesus Christ, my Lord. Amen.

J.C.S.

For further reading, see The People's Bible commentary on Exodus, pages 183-191.

Setting Earthly Skills to a Heavenly Purpose

Bible Reading: Exodus 30:1–31:11

Then the Lord said to Moses, [2] "See, I have chosen Bezalel son of Uri, the son of Hur, of the tribe of Judah, [3] and I have filled him with the Spirit of God, with wisdom, with understanding, with knowledge and with all kinds of skills." (Exodus 31:1-3)

It's challenging to talk about what our churches should look like.

Moses didn't need to select Israelites to form a building committee. The Israelites didn't cast votes on the color of the tabernacle curtains or the dimensions of the ark. The Lord left none of it to their decisions. He not only gave Moses specific instructions about *how* the tabernacle and its furnishings should be built, but he also gave specific instructions about *who* should be the ones overseeing and carrying out the work.

Not so today. Jesus is the fulfillment of all the symbolism that was on display in the tabernacle. We're free from the ceremonial laws that guided that work. As we build our churches in our place and in our time, we build them with an eye on our circumstances and abilities. While everything in our churches should still be about Jesus as they focus us on the gospel in Word and sacrament, the details are left to us. Some churches are grand and beautiful; some are small and humble. God does not give us the instructions he gave to Israel.

But there's still good reason for us to consider Bezalel and Oholiab. After giving specific directions for how to build Israel's place of worship, the Lord directed Moses to set aside Bezalel as the chief craftsman and Oholiab to be his helper. And the Lord filled them with his Spirit to give them earthly skills to work with wood and stones and to make beautiful designs. They wouldn't be preachers in the traditional sense, but God used their skills to adorn his house with beauty so that people would learn about his goodness and his glory.

Or, rather, they used God's skill to do this. It was God who gave them the ability and skill to heat and shape metal and to know how to strike a chisel and shape a stone. And he called them to put those gifts to use in his house. That's worth thinking about today. Our gifts are just that: They're gifts from God. God is glorified when we use our gifts faithfully in our homes and communities. But there's a special joy when we use our gifts to care for his house—whether large or small, glorious or humble—so that people can see reminders of God's goodness. Our talents may be earthly skills, but we can use them for a heavenly purpose.

Prayer: Lord, help me see my skills and abilities as gifts from you, and give me joy as I use them to show your glory. Amen.

J.C.S.

For further reading, see The People's Bible commentary on Exodus, pages 192-198.

God Is Serious About Rest

Bible Reading: Exodus 31:12-18

Then the LORD said to Moses, 13 "Say to the Israelites, 'You must observe my Sabbaths. This will be a sign between me and you for the generations to come, so you may know that I am the LORD, who makes you holy.'" (Exodus 31:12-13)

We need rest. We face a cost if we don't get it. Every year news reports and studies detail the ways American workers fail to get the rest we need. We have fewer vacation days than most countries, and we fail to take the ones we have. Smartphones rob us of sleep at night, and hobbies and sports steal away our weekends. Our inability to rest costs our economy billions of dollars a year in workplace accidents; poor sleep habits often cost us good health.

For the Israelites, the failure to rest would cost their lives. God's commands about the Sabbath are striking. The word *sabbath* means "rest." God commanded that every Saturday was observed as a Sabbath Day. All Israelites were to rest from work; anyone who failed to do so was to be put to death. God took rest seriously!

And with good reason. Elsewhere in Scripture, God tells us some of the purposes behind the Sabbath Day. The Sabbath was to be a day for gathering together with fellow believers for a "sacred assembly"—they would gather together to hear God's Word. They were to abstain from work so that they and their animals could have physical rest. By resting on the seventh day, they would have a weekly reminder of the God who created the world in six days and rested on the seventh. We need rest for our bodies. We need rest for our souls.

But God's design for the Sabbath wasn't just to give rest. It was to give a sign. The Lord says it twice in this chapter. Setting aside this time for rest wasn't just for the Israelites' benefit. It was a sign for the generations to come. When the Israelites would get rest for their bodies and their souls, they'd also be showing the next generation that they had been set apart by God as his holy people.

We gather for worship, we read our Bibles, and we go to God in prayer because we need the blessings he gives. But there's more happening than that. When our children—young or old—see our faithfulness in worship, when our grandchildren see our well-worn Bibles, when our neighbors see our cars driving to and from church every Sunday, God is giving the world a sign that he's still setting his people apart for him. That was God's plan for the Sabbath: rest for our bodies, rest for our souls, and a sign to the world.

Prayer: As I gather for worship and find rest for my soul, dear Lord, give a sign to the world of your gracious love. Amen.

J.C.S.

For further reading, see The People's Bible commentary on Exodus, pages 198-200.

A Golden Idol, Bloody Swords, and a Merciful Mediator

Bible Reading: Exodus 32:1–33:6

So [Moses] stood at the entrance to the camp and said, "Whoever is for the LORD, come to me." And all the Levites rallied to him. (Exodus 32:26)

Then Moses said, "You have been set apart to the LORD today, for you were against your own sons and brothers, and he has blessed you this day." (Exodus 32:29)

We often pray that God would convert others to faith in him. It's good to do that. We want people to know God's love.

But we need to remember that conversion is no small thing. When God is first in your life, everything else takes a back seat. Some things and even some people that you once loved don't just take a back seat; they become a problem, enemies, something to fight against. Conversion radically changes people's lives, priorities, and relationships.

While Moses was on the mountain with God, Aaron and the Israelites built an idol. They melted their earrings, fashioned the gold into the shape of a cow, and called it their god. Humankind's stupidity and sinfulness were on shiny display.

It's easy to focus on the Israelites' idolatry or Moses' anger as he smashed the tablets of God's law on the ground after the Israelites broke God's commandments. But that sinful scene just showcases the division that sin causes. Moses called those who stood for God to stand with him and draw their swords. He didn't hide from the pain that followed: They struck down their own sons and brothers who stood against the Lord. Standing with God brought sacrifice and loss.

But it wasn't born of hatred. Moses prayed that God would even damn his own soul if that could spare the Israelites! Moses loved God; he loved the people. But sin brings division and pain. Because the people were against God, they were against God's people. Standing with God that day was right, but it brought such pain and loss because of the sins of others.

Be like Moses. Love those lost in sin. Pray that God would forgive them and bring them to faith. But always be mindful of the change—and even pain!—God's truth brings. When we stand for what's true, we stand against what isn't. As you bring others to that truth, stand in love with them too, so they never face those challenges alone.

Prayer: Lord, work powerfully in the hearts of those who don't believe in you. Show them your truth in Christ. And show them your love in me, as I patiently support and help them in their new life of faith. Amen.

J.C.S.

For further reading, see The People's Bible commentary on Exodus, pages 200-214.

God Is Not So Far Away

Bible Reading: Exodus 33:7-23

As Moses went into the tent, the pillar of cloud would come down and stay at the entrance, while the LORD spoke with Moses. [10]Whenever the people saw the pillar of cloud standing at the entrance to the tent, they all stood and worshiped, each at the entrance to their tent. [11]The LORD would speak to Moses face to face, as one speaks to a friend. (Exodus 33:9-11)

The scene was a beautiful one: Moses walked toward a lone tent set up outside the camp of the Israelites. As he entered, a pillar of cloud descended from heaven and touched the earth at the entrance. The people knew what was happening inside: Moses was speaking to God on their behalf. The same Lord who appeared in flashes of lightning and blazing fire on Sinai was talking to Moses, as simply as you and your friend talk over a cup of coffee. And whenever Moses went to the tent, the people watched from a distance and worshiped.

But remember the context. Moses' tent for meeting with the Lord was off in the distance because of Israel's sin. Because they had worshiped the golden calf, God had told them that he wouldn't lead them into the Promised Land. He would send an angel to guide them there instead of leading them himself. Their sin had caused a separation.

Imagine the fear and sadness that separation brought the Israelites—God, gone from them? But then imagine their feelings as they watched Moses walk into the desert to meet with God and bring him their needs. God was not so far away—still within eyesight! Certainly their sin had caused problems, but God was still good and loving. And God was still close. They could see it every time Moses went to the tent.

And people can see that in you too. God can use your relationship with him to give people hope for their relationships with him. You pray, you read your Bible, and you go to church. You know that Jesus is the friend you can talk to. People who don't have that are so often like the Israelites—watching from a distance. But still, they're watching.

So let them see that God is still good. Show your joy in your faith. Eagerly pray for others. Let them see your closeness with the Lord. God can use it to show he's not so far from them either.

Prayer: What a friend I have in you, Lord Jesus. Let my friends see that too, so they may find a friend in you. Amen.

J.C.S.

For further reading, see The People's Bible commentary on Exodus, pages 214-220.

We Pass Down Sin for a While; God Passes Down Grace Forever

Bible Reading: Exodus chapter 34

[The LORD] passed in front of Moses, proclaiming, "The LORD, the LORD, the compassionate and gracious God, slow to anger, abounding in love and faithfulness, 7 maintaining love to thousands, and forgiving wickedness, rebellion and sin. Yet he does not leave the guilty unpunished; he punishes the children and their children for the sin of the parents to the third and fourth generation." (Exodus 34:6-7)

A loving couple gazes adoringly at their little daughter. Maybe they see on the child her mother's eyes or her father's smile. As she grows up, they see traces of mom's athleticism or dad's humor. We pass down traits to our children. Who we are shapes who they will be.

It goes beyond eye color and interests. Perhaps at first God sounds unfair in these verses. Punishing children for the sins of their parents? Isn't God supposed to be the judge of all the earth who always does what is right? But, of course, sin's effects are never kept in a tidy box. When a father breaks apart his family with an affair, he's not the only one who faces the pain. When a mother's decades of alcohol abuse destroy her health, her entire family is left in grief. Parents sin and their children suffer. It's a legacy we leave them.

But God isn't just describing sin's lasting effects. This is a shorter version of a thought God often expressed to Israel, that he would punish children for their parents' sin "to the third and fourth generation *of those who hate me*" (see Exodus 20:5 and Deuteronomy 5:9; emphasis added). This isn't a matter of innocent children sharing in the punishment for the sins their parents committed. This is children sharing in the sin that their parents passed down. Children see their parents ignoring God's Word or despising what he commands, and what they see shapes them just as surely as chromosomes and DNA ever could. It's a dreadful thing: Our sins can shape our families for generations to come.

We know, however, that God's grace goes further. We pass on sin. But God is faithful in forgiving it. Our lives are filled with the consequences of our actions, and our parents' and grandparents' actions as well. But God is filled with love and faithfulness. We pass on sin to the third and fourth generation. But God shows love to thousands—to countless generations. We pass on sin for a while. But God passes on his grace forever.

Prayer: Heavenly Father, by my nature I pass down my sin and its pain to those who come after me. By your grace help me pass down your forgiveness too. Amen.

J.C.S.

For further reading, see The People's Bible commentary on Exodus, pages 220-228.

Beautiful Outside and Inside

Bible Reading: Exodus chapters 35 and 36

Then the whole Israelite community withdrew from Moses' presence, [21] and everyone who was willing and whose heart moved them came and brought an offering to the LORD for the work on the tent of meeting, for all its service, and for the sacred garments. (Exodus 35:20-21)

God wants his church to be beautiful.

Moses and the Israelites didn't need to guess what the tabernacle should look like. God gave them the design. No earthly debate or decisions were necessary; there was no need for committees to fight about what color yarn should be used for the covering or how large the courtyard should be. And what God designed was beautiful! Fine wood and precious metals, beautifully colored yarns, and fine linens and leathers all combined to make a glorious place of worship.

God communicated it all to Moses and didn't spare a single detail, except where the materials should come from. God didn't list who should give what. He didn't impose a tax to gather exact amounts of gold, silver, or fabric. He didn't compel them by his law. He simply asked for gifts from whoever was willing. Who should give? Whoever wanted to. How much? However much they wanted to.

God wanted the beauty that adorned his house to be a matter of love, not a matter of law. Whenever people saw the place where God met with them, they could see reminders that this wasn't a house God had demanded from them but a house he invited them to be part of. Every thread, every bead, and every pillar was a gift of love, given only because God's love had moved people's hearts to give.

God's church isn't a matter of tents or temples. His church is all people who believe in Christ Jesus. Remember that as you adorn your life with your attitudes and actions. The beauty with which God decorates his church isn't outward acts of obedience compelled by threats of law. The beauty is hearts that have been changed by his love for us in Christ. Consider the love that God has shown to you, and let that love show through you as you seek ways to honor him and serve your neighbor. That love makes God's church truly beautiful, on the outside and on the inside.

Prayer: Heavenly Father, you have called me into your church and filled me with your Spirit. Your Son has fulfilled the law in my place and given me eternal life. Grant that the life I live reflects the beautiful love you've shown to me. Amen.

J.C.S.

For further reading, see The People's Bible commentary on Exodus, pages 228-239.

Just as Commanded, but Not Yet Complete

Bible Reading: Exodus chapters 37–39

The Israelites had done all the work just as the LORD had commanded Moses. [43]Moses inspected the work and saw that they had done it just as the LORD had commanded. So Moses blessed them. (Exodus 39:42-43)

Haven't we read all this before? When Christians commit to read the Bible from beginning to end for the first time, many start to struggle around Exodus chapters 25–30. In those chapters, God gives precise commands to the Israelites for how to build the tabernacle and its furnishings. If that doesn't derail someone's reading, these last chapters often do. In chapters 36–39, Moses gives us a detailed accounting of the Israelites' work, showing that they did everything just the way God said. If it seems repetitious, that's because it is. Moses repeats the details of the construction and constantly concludes with the refrain "just as the LORD had commanded."

What is God showing us? We can see that the Israelites learned their lesson. After the idolatry of the golden calf, they started to take God's law seriously. They tried to do everything according to his command.

Also, we can see that we should treat God's house with care and integrity. The Israelites were careful to follow the designs God gave them. They were careful with their resources and gave good accounting. And Moses blessed them for it.

Those are good lessons. But there's something more for us to see. The Israelites built what God commanded them to build in the way God commanded them to build it: Every measurement was correct, every material was chosen according to God's directions, and every artisan acted with skill. And yet it wasn't enough. It never would be. As beautiful—and as beautifully built—as the tabernacle was, it wouldn't keep the Israelites' worship life perfect; they continued to fall into idolatry. It didn't keep the preaching pure; they so often descended into work-righteousness.

Not even the best of our obedience can make us right with God. A person can memorize the Ten Commandments and understand all of Bible history. We can live disciplined lives and be faithful in our marriages. Outwardly, it may seem as if we're living just as the Lord commanded. It looks beautiful, but it doesn't provide what we need; we still stumble and fall. What we need most is our Savior Jesus. The Israelites had built the tabernacle according to God's command, but it wasn't complete. After all, it was to be a place of sacrifice—it wouldn't be complete until the Lamb was there.

Prayer: Help me, Lord, to heed your commands. And help me, Lord, to hold on to Jesus. Amen.

J.C.S.

For further reading, see The People's Bible commentary on Exodus, pages 241-247.

A Sad Ending to a Glorious Beginning?

Bible Reading: Exodus chapter 40

Then the cloud covered the tent of meeting, and the glory of the LORD filled the tabernacle. [35] Moses could not enter the tent of meeting because the cloud had settled on it, and the glory of the LORD filled the tabernacle. (Exodus 40:34-35)

Let's summarize the book of Exodus. God sees the suffering of the Israelites in Egypt. He sends Moses to deliver them. In breathtaking love, the Lord smashes the power of Egypt and carries the Israelites out of slavery as an eagle carries her young on her wings. Neither the miles of desert nor the might of enemies can stand against God's people as he gives them food and water in the wilderness and victory in the face of every foe. The Lord of heaven gathers them at the foot of Mt. Sinai as trumpets blast and lightning flashes, and he promises to be their God. At his command and with his designs, the people of Israel build a house where God might dwell in their midst, a "tent of meeting" so that God and his people can be together. With the work done, the cloud of the Lord's glory covers the tent of meeting and fills it with his presence: "God is here! God is with us!"

But they couldn't be with him. Not even Moses could enter to meet with God in that tent of meeting. And that's where the book of Exodus ends. It seems like such a sad ending to a glorious beginning. But it's not. God was about to teach his people their greatest lesson.

God is holy. Holiness is separation from sin. If God's holiness is all we see, our story will always end in sadness and separation. None of our obedience or attempts at faithfulness will ever bring us to God's holiness. We need sinlessness to stand in the presence of God. And that means we need a substitute to be righteous in our place, a sacrifice to wash our sins away. God's holiness is glorious, but we need his mercy too. Exodus shows God's power in bringing his people out of slavery, but they're left with the problem of how to draw near to a holy God. In the book of Leviticus, God opens our eyes to the answer: It's found in blood shed for sinners and righteousness given to those who don't deserve it. We'll consider those truths in the devotions to come.

Prayer: Holy Father, your holiness rightly fills me with awe and fear. Show me my Savior, my substitute and my sacrifice, that I may be filled with your love and dwell with you, now and forever. Amen.

J.C.S.

For further reading, see The People's Bible commentary on Exodus, pages 247-255.

Wholly Dedicated and Dedicated Holy

Bible Reading: Leviticus chapters 1 and 2

The LORD called to Moses and spoke to him from the tent of meeting. He said, 2 "Speak to the Israelites and say to them: 'When anyone among you brings an offering to the LORD, bring as your offering an animal from either the herd or the flock.

3 "'If the offering is a burnt offering from the herd, you are to offer a male without defect. You must present it at the entrance to the tent of meeting so that it will be acceptable to the LORD.'" (Leviticus 1:1-3)

How do you draw near to a holy God? You must be holy too.

The book of Exodus ended with the Lord's glory filling his tabernacle, but the people were unable to approach because of God's holiness. What a wonderful thing, then, that the first words in Leviticus are God calling to Moses, inviting the Israelites to draw near to him. But it would take a sacrifice.

It's easy to misunderstand the sacrifices of the Old Testament. In so many religions, sacrifices are what worshipers give to a god to make it happy. Offering sacrifices are attempts to buy a god's favor. But the sacrifices God taught the Israelites to offer were far different. They were teaching tools that showed Israel how sinners could become right with God. The first seven chapters of Leviticus give us a crash course in the four major types of sacrifices. The sacrifices weren't a way to bribe God or buy his favor. Each one was a reminder that even though the wages of sin is death, God would provide a substitute who would die in the people's place. The holy God would provide a sacrifice that would make the people holy too.

Each type of sacrifice had a different focus. Some *repaired* communion with God; some *expressed* communion with God. Burnt offerings were the latter. The animal sacrificed was burned until nothing was left; it all went up to God in the smoke. The sacrifice taught that since a holy God would make his people righteous, they could dedicate their entire lives in thankful living to him.

How do you approach a holy God? Through the sacrifice of Jesus, God has made you holy. Now dedicate your whole life to him in joy.

Prayer: Dear Savior, your sacrifice on the cross made me holy in God's sight. Help me dedicate my words, my thoughts, and my actions in thanksgiving to you. Amen.

J.C.S.

For further reading, see The People's Bible commentary on Leviticus, pages 17-29.

Our Sin, Another's Blood

Bible Reading: Leviticus chapters 3 and 4

"'[The anointed priest who sinned] is to present the bull at the entrance to the tent of meeting before the LORD. He is to lay his hand on its head and slaughter it there before the LORD.'" (Leviticus 4:4)

It can be easy to hide from the reality of sin for a while. When we confess our sins at church, we use *general* words. We acknowledge our sinfulness, and we ask God to forgive us. But we don't list specific sins out loud when we're together, and perhaps we keep those sins from even coming into our minds as we speak.

The Israelite worshiper didn't have that luxury. He didn't just drop off a lamb with a priest at the gate of the tabernacle. The sinner was personally involved with the sacrifice. The "sin offering" described in Leviticus chapter 4 was the most basic sacrifice. It was required when someone was guilty of a known sin. God told the worshiper to place his hand on the animal's head. Further specifics aren't recorded in Scripture, but rabbinic writings tell us that the sinner would confess his sin out loud, emphasizing the symbolism of his sin being laid on that animal. Then the worshiper—not the priest—would kill the animal.

It was a powerful picture. The worshiper couldn't hide from his sin, but God allowed his sin to be placed on another who would die for him. The Israelite's role in killing the animal underscored his own guilt—what shame and sadness must have been felt at that moment! But as the blood was shed, the sinner could be sure that his sins were forgiven. He had peace with God.

It can be easy to hide from our sins for a while, but we shouldn't. When we confess sins at church, the words we use are general. But as painful as it may be, we should bring our specific sins to mind. Do that, so when the pastor proclaims that Jesus died to pay for the sins of the whole world, you can know he means your sins too. When you hurt someone, don't excuse it or hide from it; confess those sins even though they bring guilt and sadness, and let the person forgive you and give you peace. When we do this, we're no longer hiding from our sins; we're remembering that Jesus shed his blood to forgive them.

Prayer: Dear Savior, I'm sorry for my sins that bring shame to you and pain to others. They trouble my heart. Give me strength to confess my sins, and help me believe that Jesus' sacrifice has given me peace. Amen.

J.C.S.

For further reading, see The People's Bible commentary on Leviticus, pages 30-44.

Making It Right

Bible Reading: Leviticus chapters 5 and 6

"If anyone sins and is unfaithful to the LORD by deceiving a neighbor about something entrusted to them or left in their care or about something stolen, or if they cheat their neighbor, [3] or if they find lost property and lie about it, or if they swear falsely about any such sin that people may commit—[4] when they sin in any of these ways and realize their guilt, they must return what they have stolen or taken by extortion, or what was entrusted to them, or the lost property they found, [5] or whatever it was they swore falsely about. They must make restitution in full, add a fifth of the value to it and give it all to the owner on the day they present their guilt offering." (Leviticus 6:2-5)

A boy is mean to his little sister and breaks her favorite toy. It's time for their father to do his job. He confronts his son with his sin and has him apologize to his sister. The sister assures her brother of forgiveness. But it doesn't stop there; it's time to make things right. The son has to dip into the money he's been saving from his past few allowances to buy his sister a new toy. As the father leads his children through this, perhaps none of the words or actions are genuine at first. But it's training; it's impressing lessons upon young hearts. A forgiven person seeks to fix the damage that he's caused. A healed heart seeks to heal the pain it's caused.

The "guilt offering" described in Leviticus chapter 6 trained Israel in the same truth. The sin offering (Leviticus 4) focused on repairing the people's relationship with God; the guilt offering focused on repairing their relationships with those they hurt. Not only would the worshiper offer a sacrifice to the Lord, but before offering the sacrifice, he would make amends to the person he harmed—even adding 20 percent where possible.

We can't always undo the earthly damages our sins cause. Sometimes the relationship is broken or the toll of sin is beyond our ability to heal. But when God allows forgiven sinners the ability to undo the harm, may we recognize that opportunity for what it is: not a sacrifice, but a gift.

Prayer: Thank you, Savior, for forgiving my sins that have caused pain and suffering for others. When possible, give me the joy of undoing the damage I've caused. When the hurt can't be repaired this side of heaven, give me faith to trust that one day you yourself will wipe away every tear and make all things new. Amen.

J.C.S.

For further reading, see The People's Bible commentary on Leviticus, pages 45-61.

This God Eats With Sinners

Bible Reading: Leviticus chapter 7

"'[Those bringing fellowship offerings] are to bring one of each kind as an offering, a contribution to the LORD; it belongs to the priest who splashes the blood of the fellowship offering against the altar.
15The meat of their fellowship offering of thanksgiving must be eaten on the day it is offered; they must leave none of it till morning.'" (Leviticus 7:14-15)

In Jesus' day, the Pharisees were shocked that Christ ate with sinners. They shouldn't have been shocked. God had been showing them this truth for more than a thousand years.

Since sacrifices pictured the forgiveness of sins, many of them were solemn and somber things. Sins were confessed, blood was shed, and restitution was made. But there was a goal for all those sacrifices: a repaired relationship with God. Peace and joy together.

The "fellowship offering" showed what that looked like. Meat and bread were brought as a sacrifice, but they weren't entirely consumed by the flames. After a portion of the meat was burned on the altar, the rest of the food was eaten by both the priests and the worshipers who brought it.

We mark our happiest occasions by sitting down for a meal with the people we love. It's a way of showing we're at peace with one another and united in love. God wanted his people to know that he didn't just accept them because their sins were washed away; he rejoiced to be with them. The picture is hard to miss!

But people still missed it. When Jesus carried out his earthly ministry, he was criticized and attacked for eating with sinners. That didn't stop him. The same Lord who taught the Israelites these truths through sacrifices gathered together with sinners for a meal on the night before he sacrificed himself for them. He forgave their sins. He rejoiced to be with them. He pointed them to the day they'd be together in heaven.

And he still gathers us together as his forgiven people. No matter what sins are in our past, he reminds us that his sacrifice washed them away. He gathers us together for Holy Communion. And he tells us that the day is coming when God will bring all his forgiven sinners home to heaven. It's not surprising to hear how he describes that day: It'll be a feast.

Prayer: Holy God, in a mystery of your love, you delight to be with sinners. You wash us clean, invite us to your table, and show your peace. Help me treasure your love that seeks to gather all people to yourself, and give me strength and courage to show that love to others. Amen.

J.C.S.

For further reading, see The People's Bible commentary on Leviticus, pages 62-68.

Set Apart for Service

Bible Reading: Leviticus chapter 8

Then Moses brought Aaron and his sons forward
and washed them with water. 7He put the tunic on
Aaron, tied the sash around him, clothed him with the robe and put the ephod on him. He also fastened the ephod with a decorative waistband, which he tied
around him. 8He placed the breastpiece on him and
put the Urim and Thummim in the breastpiece. 9Then
he placed the turban on Aaron's head and set the gold plate, the sacred emblem, on the front of it, as the LORD commanded Moses. (Leviticus 8:6-9)

What would the Israelites have seen when they looked at Aaron? They would have seen a leader who had stood by Moses' side and demanded that Pharaoh release them from slavery. A man who had held up Moses' hands so that the Lord would give the Israelites victory over the Amalekites. A miracle worker and faithful servant of the Lord in so many ways!

They would also have seen the man who had hammered their earrings into a golden idol, which had led to the deaths of so many of their brothers and sisters. Someone who had given in to bigotry as he criticized Moses for marrying a Cushite woman. Someone who had given in to such anger during their wanderings in the wilderness that the Lord would not allow him to enter the Promised Land.

How could someone like that be the high priest, serving them with God's Word? God showed them how. He had Moses wash Aaron—a symbol of forgiveness. Then Moses dressed him. As those holy robes covered Aaron and drew attention away from his *person,* God highlighted his *purpose:* The Lord set him apart and prepared him for service. It wasn't about the man. It was about the gifts that God was giving through him.

This is the same reason Christian ministers wear robes when they serve God's people. It's a message: It's not about the man; it's about the role for which God sets the man apart and equips him to carry out. The man is sinful, yes, but God sets him apart to share forgiveness. Don't let his flaws stop you from seeing God's gifts.

But the pastor isn't the only priest. You are too. God says all his people are royal priests. He doesn't give you fancy robes. Instead, he calls you to clothe yourself with compassion, kindness, humility, gentleness, and patience—with love binding them all together (Colossians 3:12-14). God gives you those gifts by his Spirit as he sets you apart to serve others. Put them on every day as a reminder: It's not about you but the gifts God gives through you.

Prayer: Lord, dress me with your gifts so that others may see your grace today. Amen.

J.C.S.

For further reading, see The People's Bible commentary on Leviticus, pages 69-79.

God's Greatest Glory Is in His Blessing

Bible Reading: Leviticus chapter 9

Then Aaron lifted his hands toward the people
and blessed them. And having sacrificed the sin offer-
ing, the burnt offering and the fellowship offering, he
stepped down.
23 Moses and Aaron then went into the tent of
meeting. When they came out, they blessed the
people; and the glory of the LORD appeared to all the
people. 24 Fire came out from the presence of the LORD
and consumed the burnt offering and the fat portions
on the altar. And when all the people saw it, they
shouted for joy and fell facedown. (Leviticus 9:22-24)

The service comes to a close. It's already been an hour—maybe a few minutes more. You know the words so well that they may not even register: "The Lord bless you and keep you. The Lord make his face shine upon you and be gracious to you. The Lord look on you with favor and give you peace." We say "amen" while we're gathering up the bulletins and our jackets. It's easy to miss what's really going on.

The people of Israel couldn't miss it. There hadn't been 60 minutes of worship; they were at the end of a seven-day worship service as Aaron and his sons were set aside as the priests of Israel. It was solemn and joyful at the same time. Sacrifices were offered for Aaron—after all, his sin was well known, and if he was going to serve, the people should see it forgiven. Blood was shed—was the Lord calling to mind Aaron's great sin at Sinai by having him offer a calf as a sacrifice? A calf of flesh and blood to atone for the calf of gold? But it was not just for Aaron; a sacrifice was offered for all the people. And Aaron was presented as the priest. Moses wasn't their only connection to God. The Lord made sure they would always have people to proclaim his grace to them. And to mark the occasion, the Lord sent fire to consume the offerings. God was with them, and it was glorious!

But it was a passing glory, a shadow of something greater. The blood of bulls and goats doesn't forgive sins. The fire of God's glory was awesome, but it was soon gone, with not even a glow remaining.

Yet for 3,500 years, Aaron's words of blessing have promised countless believers that we're not alone. Our sins don't separate us from God anymore. The Lord has accepted a sacrifice in our place, and he turns his face toward us and shines his love down on us. Don't miss it. God's greatest glory is found in his love for you.

Prayer: Almighty God, not in signs or wonders but in your Word let me find your love and your glory. Amen.

J.C.S.

For further reading, see The People's Bible commentary on Leviticus, pages 80-85.

Take Service Seriously

Bible Reading: Leviticus chapter 10

Aaron's sons Nadab and Abihu took their censers, put fire in them and added incense; and they offered unauthorized fire before the LORD, contrary to his command. [2] So fire came out from the presence of the LORD and consumed them, and they died before the LORD. (Leviticus 10:1-2)

God calls us to serve him in many different ways, but he never calls us to serve him thoughtlessly.

It was a time of incredible joy for the people of Israel. God had delivered them from Egypt and had forgiven their rebellion. He had given them instructions for worship so they could always stand in a right relationship with him. The tabernacle was constructed, the priestly robes and altars were completed, and Aaron and his sons had been consecrated for their work as priests. The Lord even showed his approval by sending fire from heaven, and the people shouted for joy when they saw it.

But the shouts of joy must have turned into screams of horror. As Aaron's sons offered incense, the same holy fire that had shown God's approval now raged forth and consumed the two men in front of everyone. As two of Aaron's sons served in worship, God burned them alive.

What did they do wrong? We don't know. There are few clues in the text. They offered "unauthorized fire." Did they offer incense at the wrong time or use coals taken from the wrong place? God almost immediately commanded that priests not drink wine while they're serving. Had Nadab and Abihu been drunk? We can't be sure of the sin, but we can be sure of this: Even though worship is to be a joyful thing, God is serious about how we do it, especially when our words and actions set examples for others.

Your vocations—the places and roles in which God calls you to serve him—are your spiritual acts of worship (see Romans 12:1). You offer your life as a living sacrifice to God. As you live your faith at work or teach your family the faith at home, you're serving as a priest of God. That's a joyous thing! But Nadab and Abihu give us a reminder: The way we go about our service both reflects how we view God and impacts how others see him. God grant that we give careful thought to both and find joy in our careful service.

Prayer: Almighty God, you set me apart to serve you with my life so others may know of your holiness and love. Help me take my life and service seriously and bless others through it. Amen.

J.C.S.

For further reading, see The People's Bible commentary on Leviticus, pages 86-92.

Unclean From the Outside . . .

Bible Reading: Leviticus chapter 11

"'These are the regulations concerning animals, birds, every living thing that moves about in the water and every creature that moves along the ground. [47]You must distinguish between the unclean and the clean, between living creatures that may be eaten and those that may not be eaten.'" (Leviticus 11:46-47)

Be careful what you take in.

The Old Testament purity laws governing what made an Israelite ceremonially "clean" or "unclean" can be taxing for a believer to read. How much more so for an Israelite to put into practice. We don't know why God allowed the Israelites to eat some animals but called others unclean. We can try to line it up with which animals are more likely to carry diseases or which ones held religious significance for pagan nations, but no explanation seems to work well. What we do know is that eating an unclean animal, or eating an animal that died in a way that caused it to be unclean, would separate an Israelite from the worship life of God's people for a time. Every single day at every single meal, the Israelites would need to be cautious about what they ate and mindful of their relationship with God.

Be careful what you take in. That's a good lesson for believers to consider today. God gives us no moral guidelines regarding what we choose to eat. But we'd do well to consider what we're "consuming." The things we take in—the shows we watch, the news we listen to at the end of each day, the articles we read—are rarely neutral. Be thoughtful about these things. Guard your heart. Seek to enjoy the blessings of God's world without fear but never without care. Be mindful of how these things impact your faith and your heart, and feast on those things that are truly good.

Prayer: Dear Savior, at my baptism you made me part of your people. You've washed away my sins and caused your Spirit to dwell within me. As I live in a fallen world, help me be mindful of what I consume. Help me avoid that which is harmful and focus on things that are pure, lovely, and praiseworthy. And when I fall, assure me that the blood you shed on the cross has made me truly clean. Amen.

J.C.S.

For further reading, see The People's Bible commentary on Leviticus, pages 93-101.

. . . And Unclean From Within

Bible Reading: Leviticus chapters 12–15

"'You must keep the Israelites separate from things that make them unclean, so they will not die in their uncleanness for defiling my dwelling place, which is among them.'" (Leviticus 15:31)

"Make sure you eat only the right kind of animals. And when you do, prepare them the right way. Take care that they haven't come in contact with anything that makes them unclean." It was a challenge, but with daily thought and extreme care, the Israelites could maybe stay free from taking in anything that made them unclean or that separated them from God and his people.

But uncleanness doesn't just come from what's around us. If the dietary laws of Leviticus chapter 11 made it hard for the Israelites to keep ceremonially clean, then chapters 12–15 made it impossible. Try as hard as they might to avoid uncleanliness, it would find them. Worse than that, it would come from within. A spot of sickness on the skin or an infection would render a person unclean. But it wasn't just signs of sickness that would do it; even the most basic life-giving functions would: A woman's menstrual cycle. A man's nighttime ejaculation. Even the birth of a child! The most personal, basic human functions left a person unclean. Separation from God didn't just come from the surrounding world; it came from simply being human.

Jesus had to reteach that lesson to the Pharisees of his day: "What comes out of a person is what defiles them. For it is from within, out of a person's heart, that evil thoughts come—sexual immorality, theft, murder, adultery, greed, malice, deceit, lewdness, envy, slander, arrogance and folly. All these evils come from inside and defile a person" (Mark 7:20-23).

It's important to remember this too. We don't guard our faith by leaving the world and seeking to filter out every last bit of wickedness. Even if we could, there's still plenty of evil that comes from within our hearts. We don't need to be hermits living in the wilderness. We need to be cleansed from within. We need to be redeemed. We need what God will show in the next section of Leviticus: someone who can make us at one with the Holy One.

Prayer: Holy Lord, God of heaven and earth, try as I might, I cannot avoid all sin or evil in this world. Evil even lives within me, though I have been baptized into your family. Grant me a sober awareness of my guilt, and give me confidence in your holy Son, who was perfect in my place. Amen.

J.C.S.

For further reading, see The People's Bible commentary on Leviticus, pages 102-133.

At-One With the One

Bible Reading: Leviticus chapter 16

"[Aaron] shall then slaughter the goat for the sin offering for the people and take its blood behind the curtain and do with it as he did with the bull's blood: He shall sprinkle it on the atonement cover and in front of it." (Leviticus 16:15)

21 "[Aaron] is to lay both hands on the head of the live goat and confess over it all the wickedness and rebellion of the Israelites—all their sins—and put them on the goat's head. He shall send the goat away into the wilderness in the care of someone appointed for the task. 22 The goat will carry on itself all their sins to a remote place; and the man shall release it in the wilderness." (Leviticus 16:21-22)

What does *forgiveness* mean?

When we hear that our sins are forgiven, the memory of their guilt still haunts us at times. While we're free from guilt, we may still carry the feeling of a guilty conscience. The earthly damage or pain doesn't instantly disappear (if ever, this side of heaven), and not all relationships become healed. We know that forgiveness changes us, but sometimes we may struggle to know exactly how.

Once a year, on what we call the great Day of Atonement, God gave his people two pictures to help them understand forgiveness. The high priest entered the Most Holy Place of the tabernacle—the one day a year he was allowed to—and sprinkled the blood of a bull on the cover of the ark of the covenant. The Lord spoke to the Israelites from above the ark, inside of which were the two tablets of God's Ten Commandments. The picture was clear enough: The blood of the bull covered the sins of the people so God couldn't "see" the sins anymore.

Then Aaron placed his hands on a scapegoat. He confessed all of Israel's great sins, symbolically transferring them to the goat. And the goat was sent far away into the wilderness. God sent the sins away.

In Hebrew it was called the Day of Covering. But an early English Bible translator understood that "covering" didn't capture everything God was doing. "Covering" and "sending away" were just the methods. The goal was for God and his people to be "at one." Since then, most English translations have called it the Day of Atonement (literally, "at-one"-ment).

God forgives you. The earthly pain may still remain; not all relationships are restored. But one relationship is completely healed. Through Jesus' sacrifice, nothing separates you from God anymore. You're at one with him.

Prayer: Heavenly Father, though the damage and pain my sins have caused may still remain for a time, help me believe that I am at one with you. Amen.

J.C.S.

For further reading, see The People's Bible commentary on Leviticus, pages 134-146.

Love Undefiled

Bible Reading: Leviticus chapters 17 and 18

"'Keep my requirements and do not follow any of the detestable customs that were practiced before you came and do not defile yourselves with them. I am the LORD your God.'" (Leviticus 18:30)

God's view of sex is entirely different from what you'll find in this world. And it's vital that we share God's view, because it's inseparably connected to how we see him.

Moses fills a chapter with "detestable" sexual practices. A few of them are still rejected in our culture, but every year it seems that more of them become socially acceptable. That shouldn't surprise us. As detestable as these practices were, they were the common practice of the nations that surrounded God's people.

The world's view of sex almost always degrades it to an act of seeking fulfillment for oneself or dominance over someone else. Get your pleasure; show your power. Intimacy is rejected; boundaries are there only to be broken as we test the limits of morality until we convince ourselves there are none. The most essential life-giving act—something that calls for trust, vulnerability, and connection—becomes a tool for war crimes, a way to break up families, a way to show that no one dictates the use of your body but you alone. That was the view of the people in Moses' day; our view is little different.

Let your faith in God renew your attitudes toward sex. Examine the rest of God's Word and you'll find a wholly different view of sex. It's in Adam's awe as the Lord brings Eve to him. It's in Solomon's delight in his wife's beauty in the Song of Songs. It's in the book of Hebrews where it tells us to honor marriage by keeping sex pure.

And all those are just echoes of what God wants us to understand. Love is a pure thing. It places others first. It doesn't ask what we can get from our neighbor but how we can serve, love, and cherish them.

No wonder God uses the relationship between husband and wife as a picture of his love for us. He loves us for our sake, not his, and he is faithful and true, even when we're not. See that pure and holy love that God has for you, and enjoy, talk about, and think about sex in a way that honors God's good gift.

Prayer: Savior, keep me from conforming to this world's fallen view of sex. Forgive my failings, and help me show your selfless and pure love in all my relationships. Amen.

J.C.S.

For further reading, see The People's Bible commentary on Leviticus, pages 149-165.

Holiness Is Unity and Separation

Bible Reading: Leviticus chapters 19 and 20

"'You are to be holy to me because I, the LORD, am holy, and I have set you apart from the nations to be my own.'" (Leviticus 20:26)

A seminary professor preached his final graduation sermon. Looking back on a lifetime of ministry, he said, "If I could do it all over again, there's one thing I'd do differently. I'd spend less time trying to get people to see what they should do and more time helping people to see who they are in Christ."

Leviticus may seem as if it spends its time telling God's people what to do. That's not the point at all. The whole book was written to help us understand the problem of holiness.

Do you think of holiness as a problem? You should. The Israelites did. They built the tabernacle, God filled it, and they couldn't enter. That's holiness. The word *holy* in Hebrew means "set apart." Separated. That's the nature of God. He's set apart and separate from sin. Follow the logic a step further and you see what that means: He's set apart from sinners. He's set apart from us.

Leviticus gives the answer to the problem, but it's not about rules. The first part of the book is about sacrifices. The sacrifices picture how God removes our sin and brings us to him. We sin, but another dies in our place. We are reunited with a holy God. This is who we are in Christ. We're forgiven, holy, and set apart from the world but united with God.

The commands are pictures of what holiness looks like. Some of them are moral: Don't do the evil things this world does! Others just drive home the point: Don't let yourself look like this evil world; be different! But following these laws doesn't bring anyone to God. The laws are reminders: This is who you are in Christ. God has set you apart. You are holy.

That is who you are in Christ. Keep seeing it. You're washed in baptismal waters, a guest at his table, united with God himself.

And you're set apart from the world. Let Paul's words ring true for you: "I urge you to live a life worthy of the calling you have received" (Ephesians 4:1). Remember that God has called you from the world to himself. And let that holiness show in your life.

Prayer: Dear Savior, let the holy life I live show the holiness you've given to me. Amen.

J.C.S.

For further reading, see The People's Bible commentary on Leviticus, pages 166-183.

Our Relationship With God Is to Be Nurtured

Bible Reading: Leviticus chapters 21–23

" 'These are the LORD's appointed festivals, the sacred assemblies you are to proclaim at their appointed times:
[5] The LORD's Passover begins at twilight on the fourteenth day of the first month.
[6] On the fifteenth day of that month the LORD's Festival of Unleavened Bread begins; for seven days you must eat bread made without yeast.
[7] On the first day hold a sacred assembly and do no regular work.
[8] For seven days present a food offering to the LORD. And on the seventh day hold a sacred assembly and do no regular work.' " (Leviticus 23:4-8)

There's an old story about a Christian man whose friend was challenging his practice of attending church regularly. The friend said, "For all the years you've been going to church, I bet you can't remember a single whole sermon that you heard."

The man considered his friend's attack for a moment and answered, "My wife's been cooking dinner for me for over 40 years. I couldn't tell you the complete menu for any of those meals. But I know this: Without those meals, I would've died a long time ago."

Faith needs to be fed and nourished, and God spread out feasts for the Israelites. After giving strict rules governing the priests and their sacrifices in chapters 21 and 22, God spends a chapter giving instructions for the "appointed festivals"—literally, the meetings between him and his people. Once a week there was a restful day of worship during which they could gather together as God's people around his Word. *Remember, the God who rested on the seventh day with a perfect Adam and Eve in the garden still wants to be with you in this fallen world.* Throughout the year there were seven major festivals, with each festival focused on a different truth about Christ's work. The spring festivals taught about Jesus' first coming; the fall festivals looked ahead to the Last Day. *Remember, the Lord is sending you a Savior to be the great sacrifice who redeems you, and God will bring you back to him.*

Every week, we gather together—not on the seventh day as in the garden but on the first day. Believers have called it the Lord's Day because Jesus rose on a Sunday. We gather in the name of the Father, the Son, and the Spirit; God still wants to be with us. And each year we walk through Jesus' life: his birth, his death, and his resurrection. We celebrate the outpouring of his Spirit on Pentecost and his promise to return on Ascension Day. Some days and services we may remember; certainly we don't remember them all. But we know what God's doing: He's giving us a feast. He's keeping our faith alive.

Prayer: Father, grant that I rejoice with those who say, "Let us go to the house of the Lord." Amen.

J.C.S.

For further reading, see The People's Bible commentary on Leviticus, pages 184-206.

Our Relationship With God Is to Be Guarded

Bible Reading: Leviticus chapter 24

Then the LORD said to Moses:
[14] "Take the blasphemer outside the camp. All those who heard him are to lay their hands on his head, and the entire assembly is to stone him.
[15] Say to the Israelites: 'Anyone who curses their God will be held responsible;
[16] anyone who blasphemes the name of the LORD is to be put to death. The entire assembly must stone them. Whether foreigner or native-born, when they blaspheme the Name they are to be put to death.'" (Leviticus 24:13-16)

I can't imagine doing it. A young Israelite man had blasphemed—he had called down curses on someone in God's name. The Lord's name, given to bring salvation, was used to wish damnation. God's response was clear: Those who had heard the curse were to place their hands on the young man, and the members of the assembly—his neighbors, his friends, his family—were to throw stones at him until he was dead. Did God really expect them to do this?

He did. It shocks us, but it's worth asking: Does it shock us so much because we value God's name so little? We're surrounded by swearing. It's become commonplace to hear little children cry out "Oh, my God" as they hear a joke on the way to a Sunday school classroom or to hear Jesus' name taken in vain for the sake of laughs on a late-night talk show. And that's the point. God's greatest gifts to us can so easily be treated as empty and worthless. It's the greatest tragedy of all. How did Jesus say it? "What good is it for someone to gain the whole world, yet forfeit their soul?" (Mark 8:36). Treating your faith as if it is nothing leads to a fate far worse than stoning.

God called for a swift and severe reaction so that the sin of one Israelite would not lead others to treat God's name as empty. God does not call us to bring capital punishment on spiritual failures like that today. But he gives us a role in safeguarding our faith and the faith of those around us. So would God have us speak up when we hear family members or people at church use God's name in vain? Would he have us apologize if we find ourselves doing so? He would—out of love for them, for those who hear them, and for God himself. And he'd remind us what the name of Jesus means: The Lord saves.

Prayer: Let me never, dear Lord, treat the most important truths as empty or meaningless. Forgive me any blasphemies you find in me, assure me of my forgiveness in Christ, and help me cherish the salvation that I find in your holy name. Amen.

J.C.S.

For further reading, see The People's Bible commentary on Leviticus, pages 207-212.

Jubilee

Bible Reading: Leviticus chapter 25

"Count off seven sabbath years—seven times seven years—so that the seven sabbath years amount to a period of forty-nine years. [9]Then have the trumpet sounded everywhere on the tenth day of the seventh month; on the Day of Atonement sound the trumpet throughout your land. [10]Consecrate the fiftieth year and proclaim liberty throughout the land to all its inhabitants. It shall be a jubilee for you; each of you is to return to your family property and to your own clan." (Leviticus 25:8-10)

"I just don't feel forgiven." Even after being assured by the person you hurt or even after hearing it declared by a pastor in worship, Christians often struggle with this feeling. We know our sins are gone, but we still feel their guilt. It's hard to let go.

God wants us to know and feel that our sins are gone. The Year of Jubilee was a special way God did this for the Israelites. Every 50th year, they were to show what forgiveness looked like. Every debt was canceled. If you previously had to sell your family's ancestral land, you received it back. Slaves were set free. People could not plant their fields; they just ate from the fruit of the land. The Year of Jubilee served two purposes: It preserved the tribal lands of Israel so the Savior could be born where God promised, and it taught about forgiveness. Forgiveness is canceled debts. Forgiveness restores what was lost. Forgiveness sets you free.

We don't know if the Israelites ever celebrated the Year of Jubilee. There's good reason to doubt they did because they often failed to celebrate even the annual Passover for long periods of time, and there's no record of a Jubilee being celebrated. It must have been hard to do so: Canceling debts comes at a cost. It seems unfair and unearned. And, of course, it is. It's *grace*, and grace is never earned.

That's why it's so important for us to show that grace is real. Forgiveness is a declaration of God's grace, but we can put it into action too. When you forgive a sin, show the person that the debt is canceled. Don't hold it over his or her head. Treat that person with love and kindness. Let your actions show that forgiveness restores what was lost. Use your actions to help that person feel what forgiveness does: It sets the forgiven free.

Prayer: Let your forgiveness, Lord, fill my life. Grant that the words we speak to one another, the songs we sing, and the way we treat one another help us feel and realize the truth that you've proclaimed: Our sins are forgiven and forgotten, and we live in your freedom. Amen.

J.C.S.

For further reading, see The People's Bible commentary on Leviticus, pages 213-224.

Blessings and Curses, but Now Only Blessings

Bible Reading: Leviticus chapters 26 and 27

"I will look on you with favor and make you fruitful and increase your numbers, and I will keep my covenant with you. 10 You will still be eating last year's harvest when you will have to move it out to make room for the new. 11 I will put my dwelling place among you, and I will not abhor you. 12 I will walk among you and be your God, and you will be my people." (Leviticus 26:9-12)

Blessings and curses—Leviticus chapter 26 is filled with them. God told the Israelites that if they were careful to keep his commands, their land would have abundant harvests, their families would grow in number, and they'd be safe from wild animals. But if they broke his laws, it didn't matter how well they plowed or fertilized—the crops wouldn't grow, and no city wall would protect them from their enemies.

Blessings for doing good; curses for doing evil. Is that how God works with you? If you can't have a baby, is it because of the time you took the Lord's name in vain? If you are careful to tithe at church, does that mean your 401(k) and your garden will grow as never before?

Not at all! These were special covenantal promises God made with the people of Israel as they waited for the Savior. To mark them as his special people, he gave them a promise that visible obedience would result in visible blessing. He hasn't given that promise to all believers of all time. In Galatians, Paul refers to the laws of Moses as a "guardian" (Galatians 3:24), or chaperone. A guardian's job is to keep a child safe until adulthood. The Mosaic Law was meant to provide protection and blessing for Israel until the Messiah came. It was limited in length, and it doesn't apply to us the same way anymore.

But the law is still meant to bring blessing to us. God doesn't promise prosperity if we keep it, but we do know his law is there for our good, protecting us and our neighbors. This is who you are as God's chosen child. This life of holiness and love is the life you were created to live, the best "you" you can be. And when you live in this way, your life will include both joys and tragedies—but never a curse. Jesus already took that away. All of your life will be a blessing.

Prayer: Forgiven by Christ, help me live according to your will, Lord, for you are good. Amen.

J.C.S.

For further reading, see The People's Bible commentary on Leviticus, pages 225-243.

The Census—It Seems as Though You Are a Number

Bible Reading: Numbers chapter 1

**All the Israelites twenty years old or more who
were able to serve in Israel's army were counted
according to their families. 46 The total number was
603,550.**
**47 The ancestral tribe of the Levites, however, was
not counted along with the others. 48 The LORD had
said to Moses: 49 "You must not count the tribe of Levi
or include them in the census of the other Israelites.
50 Instead, appoint the Levites to be in charge of the
tabernacle of the covenant law—over all its furnishings
and everything belonging to it. They are to carry the
tabernacle and all its furnishings.** (Numbers 1:45-50)

Well, that chapter was not fast reading, was it? And why would those details be important today? It is interesting that the Lord saw fit to record for us in great detail the numbers of the people of Israel being counted. What does it mean? Does it mean that the Lord looked at his people to see only numbers, especially the numbers of those men fit for military service? Could it mean that when the Lord looks at you even today, he sees only a number? That could make you feel as valuable as a customer at a crowded meat market—just standing there with your grocery cart, waiting for the person behind the counter to call out "53, what can I do for you?" as though the person really cares.

Then we take a longer look at the devotions of the past and see what the Lord is doing. Already during the years of bitter slavery, the Lord was not only preserving his people but also beginning to turn them into a mighty nation. Imagine that: Whether or not it's always noticed during the hard times, the

Lord takes care of his people and keeps his promises. Proof of that is in the numbers. You don't know which number you are, but the God of free and faithful grace who counts you as one of his own children knows. You, who are much more valuable than the numbered hairs of your head, are one of those whose sins the Lord paid for with his own blood.

The 603,550+ people of Israel could each be certain they counted because of who and what was in the center of their camp—the place where the Levites served and the priests offered daily sacrifices for the sins of the people. No matter where the people lived in the camp, they could see the smoke of the morning and evening sacrifices that forgave their sins. They could know that they counted to the Lord. So do you.

Prayer: Thank you, Lord, for counting me as one of your people and for proving your love and care with the sacrifice of the Lamb of God who takes away the sin of the world. Amen.

Jn.C.S.

For further reading, see The People's Bible commentary on Numbers, pages 13-27.

The Aaronic Blessing

Bible Reading: Numbers 6:22-27

The LORD said to Moses, 23“Tell Aaron and his
sons, ‘This is how you are to bless the Israelites. Say
to them:
24“““The LORD bless you and keep you;
25the LORD make his face shine on you and be gra-
cious to you;
26the LORD turn his face toward you and give you
peace.”’
27“So they will put my name on the Israelites, and
I will bless them.” (Numbers 6:22-27)

It used to be *gesundheit* (a German word roughly translated as “health”). Now it’s often just “Bless you!” when a person sneezes. Years ago, people said, “God bless you.”

Actually, God does bless you. This special blessing goes back to the time when Moses’ brother Aaron became the first high priest. Aaron and his descendants were given a command not to *wish* for good things for God’s people but to actually *give* good things to the people of God.

God’s people could hear those words that first came from the Lord himself. You cannot hear it in English, but you can see it in most English Bibles—the name God uses for himself in this blessing is a special name that emphasizes how he (the only true God) is the God of free and faithful grace, the God who makes promises and who will move heaven and earth to keep those promises. We see it in our English Bibles when his name is spelled in small capital letters: “the LORD.” When you hear this blessing spoken over you, know that:

- The God of free and faithful grace is protecting and providing for you on your way through life.

- The God of free and faithful grace shows his undeserved love for sinners especially by coming to you and looking at you in mercy so rich it forgives all your sins.
- The God of free and faithful grace gives you, for free, the peace that rests in the security of knowing that nothing can separate a child of God from his protection on earth and his eternal, perfect home in heaven.

Prayer: Thank you, Lord, for blessing me with life and protection, with undeserved love and forgiveness, and with peace that passes understanding, because that peace comes to me directly from you. Amen.

Jn.C.S.

For further reading, see The People's Bible commentary on Numbers, pages 60-64.

If Only You Could Be Sure!

Bible Reading: Numbers chapters 9 and 10

On the day the tabernacle, the tent of the covenant law, was set up, the cloud covered it. From evening till morning the cloud above the tabernacle looked like fire. [16]That is how it continued to be; the cloud covered it, and at night it looked like fire. [17]Whenever the cloud lifted from above the tent, the Israelites set out; wherever the cloud settled, the Israelites encamped. (Numbers 9:15-17)

The Lord gave his people so many details to follow, and through Moses he recorded exact records. There were counts, camp set-up orders, marching orders, vows, dedication directions, offerings, utensils, lighting directions, consecrations, and finally the first Passover after leaving Egypt. What was so important about those directions and that recordkeeping? It's almost like reading through the schedule of a day in a Lutheran elementary school or a training manual to care for the altar or looking at church membership records and the budget of a congregation.

Exactly. All the parts and pieces of service to the Lord are important to him, so he set things up in an orderly way, gave good directions, and kept good records—just as we still do in our congregations. It does honor the Lord, and he notices—because he watches and he's with his people. Always.

The people of Israel could see that the Lord was always with them either in the pillar of cloud that hovered over the camp by day or in the pillar of fire that hovered over the camp by night. If only you could be that certain of the Lord's presence in your life.

Well, you can be. He's promised, "Never will I leave you; never will I forsake you" (Hebrews 13:5; Deuteronomy 31:6). As amazing and as constantly visible as a pillar of cloud or fire would be, it never was the pillar itself that kept the Lord's people safe and faithful. What happened beneath the pillar was faith strengthening and soul saving. Daily sacrifices for sin were offered at the altar. There, in those sacrifices, was the promise of the coming Savior—the perfect, sinless Lamb of God—who would substitute himself for all sinners and who would once and for all time take away the sin of the world.

We who never will see the pillar of cloud or fire know that that Savior did come. Jesus is his name. And even though we don't even see him, we can be sure that he is with us. We have his promise: "Surely I am with you always, to the very end of the age" (Matthew 28:20). God's Old Testament people could always be sure. So can you.

Prayer: Thank you, Jesus, for giving me even more than a visible cloud and fire. Thank you for your written Word and the fulfilled promise of your sacrifice that has taken away my sins and made heaven my home. Amen.

Jn.C.S.

For further reading, see The People's Bible commentary on Numbers, pages 77-92.

Complaining Along the Way

Bible Reading: Numbers chapter 11

The rabble with [the people] began to crave other food, and again the Israelites started wailing and said, "If only we had meat to eat! [5]We remember the fish we ate in Egypt at no cost—also the cucumbers, melons, leeks, onions and garlic. [6]But now we have lost our appetite; we never see anything but this manna!" (Numbers 11:4-6)

What if God really answered the Lord's Prayer just the way you pray it? You know, when you pray "Give us this day our daily bread," what if that's all you got? Well, sometimes it is. But most of the time you look in the fridge or open the cupboard and you can't figure out which of all the blessings stored there will turn into your next meal. There's just too much, too many choices.

And still you find reasons to complain—just as the people of Israel did. In the wilderness there were no supermarkets, not even a corner grocery. But that wasn't a problem because every day the Lord provided his people just enough food for one more day. And it was free. Every morning they could simply walk around the camp and pick up the day's supply of food. Every day, every person had just enough of this wonderful, tasty manna that could be prepared in any number of ways. Not even their clothing or shoes wore out, yet still they found reason to complain. Kind of reminds you of, well, yourself, doesn't it? Everything in life could be a little nicer. Work could be a little easier. School could be less challenging. Friends could be more understanding. Family could be more considerate, more thankful, more loving. At least that's the way it is when we look outside of ourselves instead of at ourselves.

Grumbling and complaining come naturally from the sinful heart that infects us all. As good and gracious as the Lord is, even when he's bringing you through an illness or taking a loved one home to heaven, what he has given to you never seems like enough. Or if it was enough, it could have been a little better.

Oh, for a heart that neither grumbles nor complains, even when the Lord allows some hardship to enter your life! Such a heart is coming to you. It will be yours in the glory of heaven when you see the Lord face to face and can thank him there for blessings that came in spite of your complaining—your Savior, Jesus, forgave even that sin.

Prayer: Thank you, Lord, for blessing and preserving me, even in those times when I was ungrateful for all your gifts. Through your Word, give me a faith that even now rejoices in the blessings Jesus has prepared for me in heaven. Amen.

Jn.C.S.

For further reading, see The People's Bible commentary on Numbers, pages 92-99.

It's Not Fair!

Bible Reading: Numbers chapter 12

"Has the LORD spoken only through Moses?" [Miriam and Aaron] asked. "Hasn't he also spoken through us?" And the LORD heard this. (Numbers 12:2)

When are the events and circumstances in your life fair? That's not a difficult question. Your life is fair when things are working out for you; when you're the head, not the tail; when you have at least as much as others (maybe a little more); when the honor and respect given to you is as great as the honor and respect given to others (maybe a little more). You're not that different from Miriam and Aaron, the siblings of Moses.

But there was a difference between Moses and his siblings. The difference was not in skills or worth. The difference was in the position each held in life. Miriam was a poet and a leader of women. That's a worthwhile position. Aaron was High Priest. That's a worthwhile position. Each position had purpose and importance. Still, they were unhappy because of the position that Moses had. Moses was the Lord's appointed leader of Israel—a position of service that he carried out not for personal gain and prestige but with true humility.

You have your position in life too. Just as surely as you are in a position over some, you are in a position lower than others as well. That's actually life. And it's not always what we think is "fair." And that's okay.

It's okay because your value in life has nothing to do with your skills or worth or even your position. Your value has everything to do with the Lord's love for you. That's a love you cannot earn—it's a free gift. That's a love you do not deserve—it's given to you in spite of your failings and sins. That's a love which is not tied to anything you can do or become on earth because it's a love the Lord had for you before he laid the foundation of the earth.

Do you want to complain about the love which values you so highly that it moved God's Son to pay for your sins and give you eternal life with him? It's not fair that he did that for you. It's not something you deserve and certainly not something you could ever earn—but it is true. How wonderful that the Lord is not fair with you.

Prayer: Thank you, Lord, for the position in life you have given me, even if it is a position less than that of many others. Please help me serve you faithfully as you have gifted me to serve, and help me appreciate the faithful service of others—most of all the service of your Son as my Savior. Amen.

Jn.C.S.

For further reading, see The People's Bible commentary on Numbers, pages 100-106.

However, I Don't Believe You!

Bible Reading: Numbers chapter 13 and 14

[The spies] gave Moses this account: "We went into the land to which you sent us, and it does flow with milk and honey! Here is its fruit." (Numbers 13:27)

But the men who had gone up with [Caleb] said, "We can't attack those people; they are stronger than we are." (Numbers 13:31)

"Okay, God, it's like this: You have rescued us from a bitter slavery. You have brought us out of that slavery as conquerors, carrying clothing, silver, and gold. You have provided us with water and food while we've been wandering through the wilderness. You have fought against our enemies for us and have seen to their constant defeat. You have brought us to the very boundary of the land you promised to us and our descendants. The land that you said you would give to us flows with milk and honey. It has cities into which we can move and houses in which we can live.

"However, we don't believe you. You can't give us this land that you promised. You can't give our army victory over these powerful people. We will die with the whole army of Israel, and our children will be turned into slaves. Or, to put it bluntly, Lord, you cannot, you will not, keep your promise."

How could the people of Israel (who saw so many promises kept) make such a statement? In fact, who in their right mind would think such a thing, much less say it to the Lord Almighty, the Maker of heaven and earth?

You would. Every time you think God is not going to do what he has promised to do, every time you wonder if the Lord is really taking care of you, every time you think the Lord has forgotten about you, every time you think your life would be different if God was really in charge—you're saying, "However, I don't believe you."

There are two cures for that. The first: Go back and reread the promises the Lord has made to you. Those promises (because they are God's Word) are promises that come from the One who will not and cannot lie. Those promises are also how the Lord works—he works through his Word. So rereading each promise will increase and strengthen your confidence in that promise.

And second, stop and look at your life. The Lord has brought you safely to this new day. You may have some scars and some messy memories along the way, but he has brought you here as his own forgiven child. He has promised, and he will keep you safe.

Prayer: Thank you, heavenly Father, for giving me your words and promises. Continue to bless me as I see your faithfulness to every promise of the past so that I hang on to every promise of the future. Amen.

Jn.C.S.

For further reading, see The People's Bible commentary on Numbers, pages 106-121.

Some Lead, Others Follow

Bible Reading: Numbers chapters 16 and 17

[The men] came as a group to oppose Moses and Aaron and said to them, "You have gone too far! The whole community is holy, every one of them, and the LORD is with them. Why then do you set yourselves above the LORD's assembly?" (Numbers 16:3)

When you sandwich the truth between two lies, the lies do not become the truth.

The truth is that the Lord's people are the Lord's people. You are one of those people. You are special to the Lord, the object of his favor. He loves you. The one who used his mighty power to turn you into a believing child of your heavenly Father is the one who equips you to serve him with your life in various ways and at different times. Whatever you do as a believing child of your heavenly Father is loving service to him. But there is something that rubs against your sinful nature: In life there will always be some people who have more authority than you—some people who are above you. Sometimes it's in the church. Sometimes it's in the family. Sometimes it's in the government.

The lie is that they are going too far when they are faithfully carrying out their God-given responsibilities—even when they are carrying out those responsibilities in a way that you would not carry out those responsibilities. The lie is that they have placed themselves in a position of authority over you when it's actually the Lord who has done that himself. He calls certain believers to be leaders in the church. Those leaders may be pastors or teachers or church officers. The Lord is also the one who makes certain people to be your parents, and he's the one who gives you the leaders you have in the government.

Some lead with God-given authority. Others follow in their God-given positions. Sometimes in life you are or will be a follower. Sometimes in life you are or will be a leader. Sometimes in life you may actually be both—perhaps at different times in the same day. When the Lord makes you a leader, lead humbly and faithfully. You may not always be appreciated, but you will be faithful to your position in life. When the Lord makes you a follower, follow humbly and faithfully. You may not always be appreciated, but you will be faithful to your position in life. There's no reason to grumble in either case. After all, the Lord is the one who gives you your position in life as a member of the Lord's assembly and, in all you do, you're serving your Savior.

Prayer: Thank you, heavenly Father, for the privilege of sometimes being a follower and sometimes being a leader. In either position, give me a humble spirit that seeks to be faithful to the position in life that you have given me. Amen.

Jn.C.S.

For further reading, see The People's Bible commentary on Numbers, pages 132-146.

Be Faithful Even in Little Things

Bible Reading: Numbers chapter 20

The LORD said to Moses and Aaron, "Because you did not trust in me enough to honor me as holy in the sight of the Israelites, you will not bring this community into the land I give them." (Numbers 20:12)

These words of God record what happened in the waning months that marked the end of the Israelites' 40 years of wandering in the wilderness—and we're shocked at the lack of details. We've heard a little about the repeated rebellion and the grumbling and the complaining of God's people. We've heard a little about the relentless blessings and the protection and the providence of the Lord. And that's it!

The details God does give us are enough to remind us that we can be just as unfaithful to him as were the people who camped around the pillar of cloud by day and basked in the light of the pillar of fire by night. We also have enough detail to know that the Lord was faithful to every promise he made to his people, just as he is faithful to every promise he has made to us.

Sometimes, as he does with us, the Lord had his people wait a little while before he kept a promise. It was their opportunity to say, "This is hard, but we know the Lord will provide for us. He promised!" This time, instead of expressing their confidence in the Lord's promise of providence, the people grumbled and complained—again. The solution was another miracle. (Has anyone heard of water flowing from a rock?) The process for the miracle was simple. To display the Lord's patience and providence to the people of Israel, Aaron and Moses had to only speak to a rock in the presence of the people. Enough water would flow from that rock to satisfy the thirst of millions of people and all their livestock. The Lord was so kind and forgiving that he would graciously overlook the grumbling of the people—again.

Moses and Aaron were not so kind and forgiving. Instead of displaying the Lord's free and faithful grace, they scolded the people and pounded the rock. They thought they knew better than the Lord. They didn't. We never do, either. Moses and Aaron didn't get to enter the Promised Land of Israel. (In the end, this wasn't so tragic for these two who entered the promised land of heaven). But they teach us to trust that the Lord will accomplish what he wants in the way he wants—often using nothing but words. We honor the Lord when we trust him enough to believe that he will get done what he wants even if the only thing we do is speak his words.

Prayer: Thank you, Lord, for giving me your words. Thank you, Lord, for forgiving me when I fail to honor you just by speaking your words. Thank you, Lord, for making the promised land of heaven my eternal home—all through your Son, Jesus. Amen.

Jn.C.S.

For further reading, see The People's Bible commentary on Numbers, pages 158-165.

Well, That's Not Going to Work

Bible Reading: Numbers chapter 21

The LORD said to Moses, "Make a snake and put it up on a pole; anyone who is bitten can look at it and live." 9 So Moses made a bronze snake and put it up on a pole. Then when anyone was bitten by a snake and looked at the bronze snake, they lived. (Numbers 21:8-9)

Many children (even a lot of adults) would be spared much anguish if only a nurse would say to them: "See this big syringe in my hand and the large pointy needle at the end of it? I'm not going to stick the needle in your arm. All you have to do is look at the medicine in this syringe and your disease will go away. You'll be completely healthy."

Well, that's not going to work, is it? Everybody knows that the medicine won't work unless the needle is stuck in your arm and the medicine is injected into your body. But sometimes what we know is not accurate. Sometimes what we think is right is actually wrong. That is especially true when it comes to the plan the Lord has for saving sinners. Sinners are not saved because of what they know or because of what they think. Sinners are not saved because of what they do or because of what they do not do. Sinners are saved because of the Lord's plan and promises.

It was because of their grumbling and complaining that poisonous snakes were biting and killing the people of Israel. The only escape from certain death was a promise from the Lord: If you look at this bronze snake on a pole, the poison from the snakes will not kill you.

Well, that's not going to work, is it? But it did. It worked because the Lord made a promise and the Lord always keeps every promise he makes—even if that promise made no sense to people. Jesus talked about this promise that defeated the poison of the snakes and said this was a picture of him: "Just as Moses lifted up the snake in the wilderness, so the Son of Man must be lifted up, that everyone who believes may have eternal life in him" (John 3:14-15).

Well, that is going to work—in fact, it has worked. Jesus saved you because his heavenly Father promised that the Savior would be punished for sinners. Jesus was punished for you, and you will never be punished. In fact, because of Jesus you are blessed with eternal life instead of eternal punishment. What makes no sense to sinners is the Lord's plan and promise.

Prayer: Thank you, Jesus, for suffering the punishment I deserve for my sins. Thank you for giving me eternal life. Amen.

Jn.C.S.

For further reading, see The People's Bible commentary on Numbers, pages 165-171.

What Can't Be Stolen Can Be Thrown Away

Bible Reading: Numbers chapters 22–25

"I see him, but not now; I behold him, but not near.

A star will come out of Jacob; a scepter will rise out of Israel." (Numbers 24:17)

"A ruler will come out of Jacob." (Numbers 24:19)

Almost!

The Israelites had reached their final stop in what had become a 40-year journey from slavery in Egypt to the Promised Land. Forty years earlier they had lost the privilege of marching into that land as conquerors who would live in houses they did not build and eat crops they did not plant. Because they had refused to believe that the Lord would give them what he had promised, they lost the privilege for 40 years.

Now the enemies of Israel thought they could use some vile, hybrid mixture of the Lord's name and Satan-inspired, occult practices to steal the Lord's blessings from his people and replace those blessings with curses. That didn't work. That couldn't work. The Lord does not leave and will not forsake his people. The promises he has made will be kept. The protection he offers will not fail. The devil himself cannot cause the Lord's promises to be changed.

But sometimes the Lord's own people are tempted to throw away what cannot be stolen from them. That happened as the people were now camped on the banks of the Promised Land. The evil unbelievers, Balaam and Balak, discovered that they could not manipulate the Lord for any amount of money or with any false worship. So what Balaam and Balak could not accomplish with their sins, they tempted many Israelites to throw away on their own. Balaam (so we're told in Numbers 31:16) incited the Israelites to be unfaithful to the Lord. Many of the Israelites believed the lie that the gods of the Midianites and Moabites were as good as the Lord God who had brought them safely to the Promised Land. They believed the lie that evil can be good if it's done in the name of the Lord or if it's called worship.

The Lord's judgment against the evildoers was swift as he once again reminded his people that he will not tolerate unfaithfulness because of the harm that it does. Thanks to the faithfulness of some of the people, the nation was spared. Better than that, in the middle of all this intrigue and unfaithfulness, the Lord renewed the promise of the Savior. Jesus, the Savior, would come out of Jacob; the Savior would be a King who would rule, just as the Lord promised.

Prayer: Thank you, heavenly Father, for reminding me that evil is always evil, no matter what it is called or how it is disguised. Preserve me from such temptations, even as (for Jesus' sake) you forgive my many transgressions. Strengthen my faith, and guide and guard my life so that I am not tempted to throw away the blessings you have in store for me. Help me serve you faithfully. Amen.

Jn.C.S.

For further reading, see The People's Bible commentary on Numbers, pages 172-191.

Everyone Counts

Bible Reading: Numbers 26:1–27:11; chapter 36

The Lord said to [Moses,] [7]"What Zelophehad's daughters are saying is right. You must certainly give them property as an inheritance among their father's relatives and give their father's inheritance to them." (Numbers 27:6-7)

The 40 years in the wilderness had accomplished their purpose. Only two of the 12 spies (Joshua and Caleb) were left of the men counted in the first census taken 40 years earlier. The rest of those over 20 years old had grumbled against the Lord and had rejected the glowing report of Joshua and Caleb. After spying out the land, those two had proclaimed that the land was flowing with milk and honey, just as the Lord had said, and they had been positive that the Israelites would take possession of the land—because the Lord said that they could and that they would.

All the rest of the spies, fearing the inhabitants of Canaan, had said the people of Israel could not defeat those powerful Canaanite people. The Israelites had been convinced that they would be killed and that their children would become slaves. They refused to even try to go in. They got what they wanted. The Lord said that they could not go in. In fact, they would all die during the next 40 years of wandering in the wilderness. Their children, however, would take possession of the land.

Now, once again, God's people stood at the border. It was time once more to move into the Promised Land. So that everything could be done in an orderly way, there was a second census. Each tribe would receive a portion of the land in keeping with the population of that tribe. In absolute fairness, the Lord decided to give them their shares through a process of casting lots. Everyone could be happy because they were receiving a right-sized portion of the land promised to the whole nation. The land that each tribe received would be an inheritance for their family to keep.

Because everyone counted, the Lord gave orders that the daughters of Zelophehad (Zelophehad had no sons) would receive their father's share of the land. Because everyone counted, the Lord's standing law for Israel was that the daughters (or the nearest relatives) should receive any assigned inheritance. That would safeguard the family name and inheritance.

Those whom many people may overlook are those whom the Lord cherishes and protects. Because he is always faithful to every promise, none of the children of the Israelites would become slaves and none of their daughters would be deprived of a family inheritance. That same faithfulness to details is the Lord's commitment to you. Not one of his promises to you will fall to the ground unfulfilled. Best of all is your inheritance in the promised land of heaven—it's Jesus' promise to you as a forgiven child of your heavenly Father.

Prayer: Thank you, Father, for not overlooking any of my needs, no matter how insignificant I may be to the rest of the world. I'm eager for my permanent inheritance in heaven. Amen.

Jn.C.S.

For further reading, see The People's Bible commentary on Numbers, pages 191-200, 245-247.

Who's Watching the Sheep?

Bible Reading: Numbers 27:12-23

Moses said to the LORD, [16]"May the LORD, the God who gives breath to all living things, appoint someone over this community [17]to go out and come in before them, one who will lead them out and bring them in, so the LORD's people will not be like sheep without a shepherd." (Numbers 27:15-17)

Sheep are not very smart; they're not very strong; they're not self-sufficient. They are apt to wander off if no one's in charge. They easily get into trouble when left unattended or uncorralled. They are defenseless against wolves and bears and lions. They need guidance and help in finding (and not polluting) sources of food and water. Maybe that's why the Lord often compares his people to sheep and gives us examples of what good shepherds do.

Great Old Testament leaders such as Moses and David learned to lead when they served as shepherds. The Lord describes his prophets as shepherds. It was to shepherds, watching over their flocks at night, that the angel announced the birth of the Savior in Bethlehem. Your Savior Jesus emphasizes his loving care for you when he compares himself to a faithful shepherd— the kind who leads and feeds and waters and defends the sheep in his care. Jesus, your Good Shepherd, is also sad when he sees his people wandering around without a faithful leader. He compares those believers to sheep without a shepherd. Moses did the same.

Moses knew that he would be unable to personally lead the people of Israel into the Promised Land. He knew that he had lost the privilege when he had failed to honor the Lord by simply speaking (as the Lord had commanded) to make water gush from a rock. Moses also knew that the Lord's people still needed someone to care for them and lead them once they crossed the Jordan. So Moses prayed. He prayed for a God-appointed leader (a shepherd) who would lead the people in the way that the Lord wanted his people to be led.

The Lord answers similar prayers today when he provides congregations with pastors (the word *pastor* means "shepherd") to lead them and when he provides teachers to shepherd their children in Christian grade schools, high schools, colleges, and pastor-training seminaries.

Sometimes when the Lord has us wait for him to provide such blessings, we realize how wonderful it is to have faithful shepherds to lead and feed and train and defend us with the Word of God. It's a blessing to have someone watching the sheep.

Prayer: Thank you, heavenly Father, for appointing those whom you want to shepherd me and others with the truth of your Word. Continue to lead faithful Christians into the public ministry and provide them as leaders in our churches and schools. Bless me in my life as I follow the faithful shepherds you give to me. Amen.

Jn.C.S.

For further reading, see The People's Bible commentary on Numbers, pages 200-216.

Where's the Blood?

Bible Reading: Numbers chapters 28–30

"' . . . all without defect.'" (Numbers 28:19)

Moses told the Israelites all that the Lord commanded him. (Numbers 29:40)

The Lord once more reviewed the sacrifices he established for the worship that could take place only at the tabernacle (the portable tent of worship used during the years of wandering in the wilderness) and finally at the temple in Jerusalem. Moses gave all the details of the sacrifices to the Israelites one more time. It was important information because it was the way the Lord said his people were to worship him. This worship was not easy (hard work and exacting directions were involved). This worship was also not cheap. The Lord would accept only the best from his people—sacrifices that had no defect. And this worship required a lot of animals, plus grain offerings and drink offerings. In the course of a year, 1,273 animals were sacrificed: 1,093 lambs, 113 bulls, 37 rams, and 30 goats.

In the mid-1800s, a young Jewish boy was paying close attention to the worship at the local synagogue. The worship there and the Lord's Word he heard started his journey to Christianity. As the sacrifices were discussed but not carried out, he turned to his mother and asked, "Where's the blood?" He knew that 1,273 animals could not be sacrificed without a lot of blood—and there could be no blood at the synagogue because it was not the temple in Jerusalem. The blood was important because the Lord had taught his people that without the shedding of blood, there is no forgiveness of sins.

When the blood of these animals was shed (and the animal died), it was a daily reminder that the wages of sin is death. It was also a reminder that there could be a substitute (a lamb of God) which could not only carry the sins of the people but also die because of those sins. The bleeding and suffering and dying of the animal that had no defect of its own was a picture of the bleeding and suffering and dying of Jesus, the sinless Son of God who died because of sins that were not his own. Jesus was charged with your sins. He suffered God's punishment for all your sins. He died because of your sins. His blood has washed away all our sins. Because of Jesus, the Lamb of God, you are forgiven. For the people of Israel, the sacrifices pictured the Savior who was coming in the future. You know the Savior did come. Because Jesus not only suffered and died but also rose from the dead, you can look forward to a perfect, everlasting life in heaven.

Prayer: Thank you, Jesus, for the Old Testament pictures that pointed to your perfect sacrifice for the sins of the world. Thank you, Jesus, for forgiving my sins and for giving me eternal life. Amen.

Jn.C.S.

For further reading, see The People's Bible commentary on Numbers, pages 204-216.

Vengeance Is Godly

Bible Reading: Numbers chapter 31

The LORD said to Moses, 2 "Take vengeance on the Midianites for the Israelites. After that, you will be gathered to your people." (Numbers 31:1-2)

Maybe more often than not, people think that vengeance is wrong because they mistakenly think that vengeance is "getting even" with someone. That's not correct. Vengeance is inflicting punishment on those who have done wrong. It's important to remember, however, that the punishment is supposed to be delivered by someone who has the authority to administer it. No individual gets to hand out the punishment an evildoer has earned, and no one gets to guess that someone should receive a punishment. Only guilty people are to be punished for the evil they have done. Only those who have the God-given duty to do so are to hand out punishment to the guilty.

The Midianites were a guilty people, responsible for a great evil. They had successfully tempted many of God's people to turn away from him when his people were just about to enter the land that he had promised to them. The Midianites (at the instigation of the money-hungry, false prophet Balaam) had convinced the Israelites to become involved in a mixture of idolatry and adultery. Those Israelites joined the Midianites in all kinds of horrible evil. They convinced the Israelites that evil was good, that one god was as good as another god, and that sin could be a good thing to do if that sin was committed under the name of worship. The result was that 24,000 Israelites lost their lives because of their unfaithfulness to the Lord and his Word.

Now it was time for the Lord to pass out the punishment that the Midianites deserved. So before Moses passed leadership of the Israelites to Joshua, the Lord used Moses and the Israelite army as his instruments to deliver punishment. Those individuals would be involved in this important work, but they would be acting at the Lord's direction and with the Lord's authority. The Lord acts in a similar way when he uses the government he has established to pass out punishment on those who have violated the law.

God's judgment was swift and complete. All the Midianites involved in that evil treachery against the Lord and his people were executed. Only the innocent survived.

Prayer: Thank you, heavenly Father, for establishing order in society so that evil can be punished and good can be protected and rewarded. Please give us a good and responsible government that will faithfully, accurately, and speedily defend those who need to be defended and punish those who do wrong. In the peace of such a society, use us to teach others what is evil and what is good. Bless us with your peace. Amen.

Jn.C.S.

For further reading, see The People's Bible commentary on Numbers, pages 217-224.

All for One; One for All

Bible Reading: Numbers chapter 32

"We will not return to our homes until each of the Israelites has received their inheritance." (Numbers 32:18)

It happens in every family because every family is made up of sinners. Family members disappoint one another. Sometimes they squabble. Other times they hurt one another's feelings. But in the end, faithful family members stick together. They help one another. They defend one another. They depend on one another.

All that was true for the people of Israel too. They had their family difficulties in the last 40 years, but now they were going to enter the Promised Land (the area east of the Mediterranean Sea and west of the Jordan River). God promised that they would take possession of it, but they had some war to wage first. God was going to use them to carry out his judgment upon the unbelieving Canaanites who lived in the land. The Canaanites were evil people. They had become so morally corrupt that some of their "worship" involved murdering their own children and burning their bodies. Other parts of their "worship" involved sexual immorality for both men and women. Their evil had become so widely accepted that the Lord could not tolerate it any longer. He decided to use his people to end that sinful "worship" by eliminating those nations. In the end, the people of Israel would then live in houses and cities they did not build, and they would harvest crops they did not plant. All of that would be God's gift to them as they conquered the Canaanites.

The problem was that two and a half tribes (Reuben, Gad, and half of Manasseh) wanted to stay on the east side of the Jordan River, where the land and cities were ideal for raising livestock—the way of life for those tribes. But the Canaanite enemy lived on the west side of the Jordan, and a large army was needed to defeat the Canaanites. That meant the help of the tribes of Reuben, Gad, and half of Manasseh was important. Because they were family, these tribes committed to crossing the Jordan and fighting shoulder to shoulder with the other nine and a half tribes. In fact, they refused to return home until the victory was won. All for one and one for all.

The Lord gave them that victory, not only because he promised that the land would be theirs but also because he promised that the Savior would be born in that land. It took about another 1,400 years, but when the time was right, Jesus was born. He was the one who came to save all.

Prayer: Thank you, Lord, for your faithfulness to all your promises. Bless my study of the history of your people so that I constantly see in it your faithfulness to your promises—the best and most important being the promise of my Savior, Jesus. Amen.

Jn.C.S.

For further reading, see The People's Bible commentary on Numbers, pages 225-230.

Be Careful to Remember and Repeat

Bible Reading: Deuteronomy chapters 1–4[1]

Only be careful, and watch yourselves closely so that you do not forget the things your eyes have seen or let them fade from your heart as long as you live. Teach them to your children and to their children after them. [10]Remember the day you stood before the LORD your God at Horeb, when he said to me, "Assemble the people before me to hear my words so that they may learn to revere me as long as they live in the land and may teach them to their children." (Deuteronomy 4:9-10)

Each one of these devotions has had a suggested Bible reading to go along with it. This time, it's Deuteronomy chapters 1–4. It's worthwhile reading, and it'll give you a sense of what the book is about. Deuteronomy ends the Pentateuch—the five grand books of Moses that God uses to begin the Bible—with a review of the Israelites' relationship with God from the time they were camped at Mount Sinai until the moment they were about to enter the Promised Land.

God told them to be careful to remember the past and to tell it to their children. What would they talk about? Worshiping golden calves and needing bronze snakes. Decades of wandering caused by their complaining. Countless problems caused by their faithlessness. And God's grace in forgiving them, picking them up, and still guiding them on. "Be careful to remember these things. Be careful to repeat them to your children. Then your children will learn."

---

[1]The book of Deuteronomy is often called the "second giving of the Law" and reiterates much of what Moses has said before. The authors of these devotions have chosen to focus on some of the major themes of this book as subjects for our meditation. –ed.

Spend time thinking about that, and do the same for your children and grandchildren. Don't just tell them what Jesus did when he died on the cross. Tell them how God brought Jesus' grace to you. Let them know about your sins and failures, your stumbles and your fears, and God's grace in it all: the pastor who taught you, the parents who forgave you, the church family who strengthened you. Tell them about God's grace and love in your life. Be careful to remember those things and repeat them to the next generation. Tell them what God did for you, and they'll understand that he's there to do it for them too.

Prayer: Heavenly Father, help me see my life as the story of your real grace and love in action, and bless my words as I tell the story to others. Amen.

J.C.S.

For further reading, see The People's Bible commentary on Deuteronomy, pages 17-60.

Remember and Relay God's Will

Bible Reading: Deuteronomy chapters 5–26

Hear, O Israel: The LORD our God, the LORD is
one. 5 Love the LORD your God with all your heart and
with all your soul and with all your strength. 6 These
commandments that I give you today are to be on your
hearts. 7 Impress them on your children. Talk about
them when you sit at home and when you walk along
the road, when you lie down and when you get up.
8 Tie them as symbols on your hands and bind them
on your foreheads. 9 Write them on the doorframes of
your houses and on your gates. (Deuteronomy 6:4-9)

The Holy Spirit uses God's Word to create faith in hearts. That's his "means." But that Word never operates in a vacuum. The Spirit uses people. He uses opportunities. He uses time.

Look at the verbs that fill God's great command to train the next generation: *impress* them; *talk about* them as you sit, walk, lie down, and get up; *tie* them; *bind* them; *write* them. This isn't just the work of Sunday morning worship or an annual week of vacation Bible school. This is discipleship. It's an all-day, everyday task.

If you see that as a frightening thought, step back and look again. Does it ever seem as if your children will never really "get" what you're trying to teach them about God's will for their lives? After years, do you still struggle and fall? Does your family feel like a constant work in progress? That's because it is. We can't learn these things overnight. Life constantly teaches us to doubt God's law; our sinful nature always pulls us toward rebellion. We can think of a hundred ways our will is better than God's, no matter how many thousands of times we've suffered pain from choosing our own paths. Will we ever learn?

We won't be perfect on this side of heaven, but we can learn and grow. We must. We're disciples of the Lord. Don't give up—after all, the Lord doesn't. And remember to relay those truths to others. God's given you what you need. It just takes opportunities, time, and, above all, his Word—the Spirit will do his work.

Prayer: Lord, throughout my life you've trained me. Be with me as I train others in your truth. Amen.

J.C.S.

For further reading, see The People's Bible commentary on Deuteronomy, pages 60-241.

Remember and Repeat God's Covenant

Bible Reading: Deuteronomy chapters 27–30

> **See, I [Moses] set before you today life and prosperity, death and destruction. [16]For I command you today to love the LORD your God, to walk in obedience to him, and to keep his commands, decrees and laws; then you will live and increase, and the LORD your God will bless you in the land you are entering to possess.** (Deuteronomy 30:15-16)

What are you going to pass on to your children?

It's hard not to think about that when you read through Deuteronomy. It's what Moses was doing. He'd been Israel's surrogate father for the last 40 years. He was now getting ready to die. He was not being misty-eyed or sentimental. He was carrying out his fatherly duty one last time and giving his children what they needed. He reminded them of their history. He repeated God's system of laws that would guide and govern them. But this was never about the past or the present. It was about life and death—their very relationship with God.

Parents often work so hard to raise their children with good Bible knowledge; bedtime Bible stories are read every night. And they work to teach their children what it means to live a godly life. Lessons are bound on their children's hearts as they walk along the road. Those things are wonderful, essential. Pass on those things.

But it's God's covenant, our relationship with him, that's at the heart of it. A covenant is a promise. The one Moses passed on was unique: God promised to watch over their nation *as long as* they were faithful to him. He had made that promise to Abraham. He had sealed it for the Israelites at Mount Sinai. He set it before them again now as they entered the Promised Land. He had to keep repeating it. The Israelites broke it again and again!

You get to pass on a different covenant. God promises to be our God, even when we fail. He promises to wash our sins away in the blood of Christ, no strings attached. It's still all about life and death. Now it's just about Jesus' death, and it gives us life. Treasure that and you'll always be blessed. Pass that on and your children will be blessed too.

Prayer: Dear Lord, your death is my life. Your sacrifice is what unites me to you. As I shape and raise those who would come after me, help me give them more than a life story or a lifestyle. Help me give them life. Help me give them you. Amen.

J.C.S.

For further reading, see The People's Bible commentary Deuteronomy, pages 248-289.

Remember and Repeat, Because the Lord Is Faithful

Bible Reading: Deuteronomy chapters 31–34

"There is no one like the God of Jeshurun, who rides across the heavens to help you and on the clouds in his majesty. 27 The eternal God is your refuge, and underneath are the everlasting arms." (Deuteronomy 33:26-27)

"Blessed are you, Israel! Who is like you, a people saved by the LORD?" (Deuteronomy 33:29)

From Adam to Abraham to Moses to Joshua, God had worked all things to bring the Israelites to the border of the Promised Land. Through their centuries of slavery and their decades of wandering—despite the adulteries of the patriarchs and the idolatries of the Israelites—the Lord had been preparing his people for just this moment. They were about to enter the land where God would make them a great nation and through them send a Savior for the world. You might think this great chapter of Israel's history would close with nothing but excitement and joy because a bright future was coming!

You may think this if you hadn't paid attention to their history—or understood your own heart. As they prepared to enter the Promised Land, God instead told Moses and Joshua that when the Israelites entered the new land and enjoyed God's blessings, they'd soon forsake him and break his covenant—again. It was a sobering prediction of Israel's faithlessness. But not just that: It was a promise that their faithlessness would never stop God from being faithful.

The first devotion in this book noted that Genesis chapter 1 was a good beginning that spoke of a good God. The world is a far different place than the perfect world God created. You can see it when you look around. You can find it when you look within too. We realize our sinfulness all the more as we read God's Word. But in his Word we also find the only answer to our sin problem: God's faithfulness overcomes our faithlessness. That's still the story of his work in our lives and his promise to us in Christ. That's why we remember it. That's why we repeat these truths. We're part of a good God's story, and his faithfulness will never fail.

Prayer: In my victories, O Lord, and in my failures, give me comfort in the promise of your great faithfulness, and hold me always in your everlasting arms. Amen.

J.C.S.

For further reading, see The People's Bible commentary on Deuteronomy, pages 291-347.

People's
Bible
Devotions

Look for these other titles in the People's Bible Devotions series:

Old Testament

From the Beginning: God's Salvation Plan
Being the People of the Promise
Faithful God, Flawed Followers
Wisdom and Folly
Hope in Dark Times
God Has a Word for You

New Testament

He Is the Christ
The Gospel Knows No Boundaries
I Want to Know Christ
Until Christ Comes: Passing on the Gospel
You Are God's Special Possession
We Have Seen His Glory

Scan to view the series

"En nuestro lenguaje moderno, el 'temor del Señor' no tiene una connotación positiva. No suena como un término que inspire vida. Evoca la idea de acobardarse en turbación bajo algo terrible. El temor del Señor es el principio de la sabiduría, de modo que es esencial que los creyentes comprendan lo que Dios quiere decir y lo que no con esa frase. Christina nos guía a través de las Escrituras a entenderla tal y como Dios la aplica. Christina es una guía capaz, y la lectora se beneficiará de su mirada cuidadosa y exhaustiva de las Escrituras que hablan del temor del Señor".

Wendy Alsup, madre, maestra de matemáticas y autora de *Companions in Suffering: Comfort for Times of Loss and Loneliness*

"Todas luchamos con el temor y necesitamos abrazar las verdades consignadas en estas páginas. El texto claro y cercano de Christina nos invita a ver más allá de nuestros temores y a dirigirnos al amor que el Señor tiene por nosotras. Ella nos enseña dulcemente a lanzarnos al propósito de crecer en nuestra reverencia y asombro del Señor, y a encontrar así consuelo en Él".

Darby Strickland, consejera CCEF, maestra y autora de *Is it Abuse? A Biblical Guide to Identifying Domestic Abuse and Helping Victims*

"Durante los momentos de prueba o dificultad, rara vez dedicamos tiempo a analizar el temor que se oculta detrás de nuestro enojo, frustración o ansiedad. Sin embargo, el hecho de confrontar esos temores menores con el temor supremo del Señor, quien nos ha prometido su presencia, cambiará el rumbo de cada situación. *Un temor santo* ofrece esa perspectiva bíblica tan necesaria. Sus páginas brindan ricos principios del evangelio que nos permiten combatir nuestros temores menores y reemplazarlos con un temor del Señor que nos anima a vivir sabiamente".

Karen Hodge, coordinadora de los ministerios de la mujer para la Presbyterian Church in America (PCA) y autora de *Transformed: Life-taker to Life-giver and Life-giving Leadership*

"Christina Fox invita a las lectoras a pisar suelo santo, maravilladas ante la perfección absoluta de la naturaleza de Dios. Y no se queda ahí, sino que conduce a quienes temen a Dios de la cima gloriosa a la vida práctica y cotidiana. Te advierto: *Un temor santo* encogerá tus temores menores y motivará una profunda adoración y devoción al Dios glorioso que nos hizo para que seamos suyas. No hacen falta zapatos para emprender este peregrinaje transformador bajo la guía de una viajera experimentada".

Leslie Bennett, directora de proyectos de los ministerios de la mujer, Revive Our Hearts [Aviva Nuestros Corazones]

"¿Sorprende señalar que vivimos en un mundo lleno de temor? ¿Cuál es la respuesta del cristiano frente a culturas que buscan atizar esos temores? Christina Fox nos muestra que la respuesta al temor del mundo es el temor correcto: el temor del Señor. Este libro es una ayuda excelente para comprender lo que es y cómo este temor que conviene puede guardarnos de vivir llenos de temor. Lo recomiendo encarecidamente".

Ike Reeder, presidente de Birmingham Theological Seminary

"Este libro no podría haber llegado en un mejor momento. Cada día nos levantamos y encontramos informes noticiosos y publicaciones en las redes sociales que llenan de temor nuestro corazón. Nuestros vecinos están preocupados por la economía, la salud, la seguridad y la estabilidad. Nosotras también. Afortunadamente, Christina Fox reorienta nuestro corazón en las páginas de este libro. En vez de temer los afanes cotidianos de la vida en un mundo caído, nos señala nuestra necesidad de cultivar un temor santo del Dios eterno que rige el universo. Solo si tememos a Dios como conviene descansaremos de todos los demás temores que podamos experimentar. Y al temer a Dios hallaremos vida abundante. Con una teología rica, una diligente exposición bíblica y valiosas preguntas de estudio, *Un temor santo* te llevará de la mano al lugar de seguridad y estabilidad que todas deseamos".

Megan Hill, autora de *A Place to Belong: Learning to Love the Local Church*, editora de Coalición por el Evangelio y esposa de pastor

"Todos los seres humanos tenemos temores y estamos motivados por nuestros temores. A su manera, nuestros miedos nos impulsan y dirigen. Lo que Christina Fox logra tan bien en este libro es abordar la realidad de nuestros temores, diagnosticar su fuente y recetar la solución. En su libro verás que el remedio para nuestros temores es el temor, porque el problema de raíz en el corazón de cada ser humano no es *el hecho de que* tememos, sino *aquello que* tememos. O, dicho con mayor claridad, *a quién* tememos".

Tim Challies, bloguero, Challies.com